Spring Tides
Memories of Alaskan Towboats

By Ed Larson
Illustrations by the author

The term "spring tide" does not allude to the season of the year. Rather, the word spring is used to designate those greater tidal ranges created when the moon is in its new or full phase.

There is a tide in the affairs of men,
Which, taken at the flood, leads on to fortune;
Omitted, all the voyage of their life
Is bound in shallows and in miseries.

Shakespeare

Julius Caesar

Copyright © 1996 by Edward Larson

All rights reserved. No part of this publication may be used or reproduced in any manner whatsoever without written permission except in the case of brief quotations embodied in critical articles or reviews.

Cover design and illustrations by the author
first printing, September 1996

10 9 8 7 6 5 4 3 2 1

First publication by
Edward Larson 228 16th. Avenue
Santa Cruz, CA. 95062
Library of Congress Catalog Card Number 96-94798

ISBN 0-9654376-0-4

Dedication

*This be the verse you grave for me: "Here he lies where he longed to be;
Home is the sailor, home from the sea, And the hunter home from the hill."*
                                        Requiem, *Robert Louis Stevenson*

Oscar Andrew Larson 1890-1971

He loved and adopted another man's child. Many of the good things I know of life, he taught me...how to fish, the importance of knowing boats and the sea, how to tie a bowline and how to treat others. I am profoundly grateful to this man, the only father I ever knew.

Dr. Charles D. Rehm 1920-1996

During the course of this writing, my uncle succumbed to a serious disease. Mentioned prominently in this book, he was, in all ways, my brother. A man of principle, integrity and wisdom, we shared the adventure of Alaska and a deep and profound affection.

Launching Data

Please imagine we had built a boat instead of a book. At the completion I would assemble my fellow workers about me, share a glass, and ask their assistance in knocking out the blocks and sending her down the ways. There would be joy and a great clapping of hands as the hull met the sea. With a book it's different; one fades a little troubled into its ending, leaning back at last in the chair assailed with the disquieting suspicion that a bronze screw here or there may still be untightened. So be it.

I was privileged to work with a strong and able crew whose words, advice, and memories assembled this craft from keelson to truck. I am deeply grateful to them all.

My deepest thanks go to Phil Hastin, my dear shipmate of so many years ago—and to Bob Morgan, Bob Thorstensen and David Lyon who laid the keel and adzed it down to proper taper, and to Stan Tarrant whose advice and suggestions sharpened the tools and laid the garboard stakes.

My thanks also to Lee Makovich, an accomplished writer, and to Ralph M. Bartholomew whose photos and words helped lay the ribs and set the knees—both share the heady wine of wooden hulls and memories.

My thanks to Phyllis Buschmann and her son, Glen, whose kindness and expertise planked the hull, and to the critical proofing of Sharon Bandy and Pat Murchison whose quips and paper clips fastened it with fine bronze. Frank Nolan Jr. drilled the limber holes with his friendship and facts, and Nick Floratos, my dear partner of nearly forty years, will buy the first copy--at full retail, of course.

Barbara Brandmier's photographs and reminiscence drove the oakem with the broad steel chisel of remembrance of the Port Althorp times we shared over half a century ago, while Don Franett, my old boss at Waterfall, with photos and words, brushed the "copper ole" across the finished hull.

My thanks also to Jim Johnson, who constantly pushed and pulled at my computer, thus laying the deck beams and stepping the mast. There were others, close aboard or hull down beyond the horizon, who swept the shavings or fired the steam box—my gratitude to all.

And finally, my love and thanks go to my wife, Marilyn, the engine of this craft. Through two years of labor, understanding and faith, she never needed oil or skipped a beat. Without her help and devotion, this launching would never occur. I give to her the bottled champagne with all expectations that she will smash it firmly against the stem iron of this craft and send it on a fabled voyage.

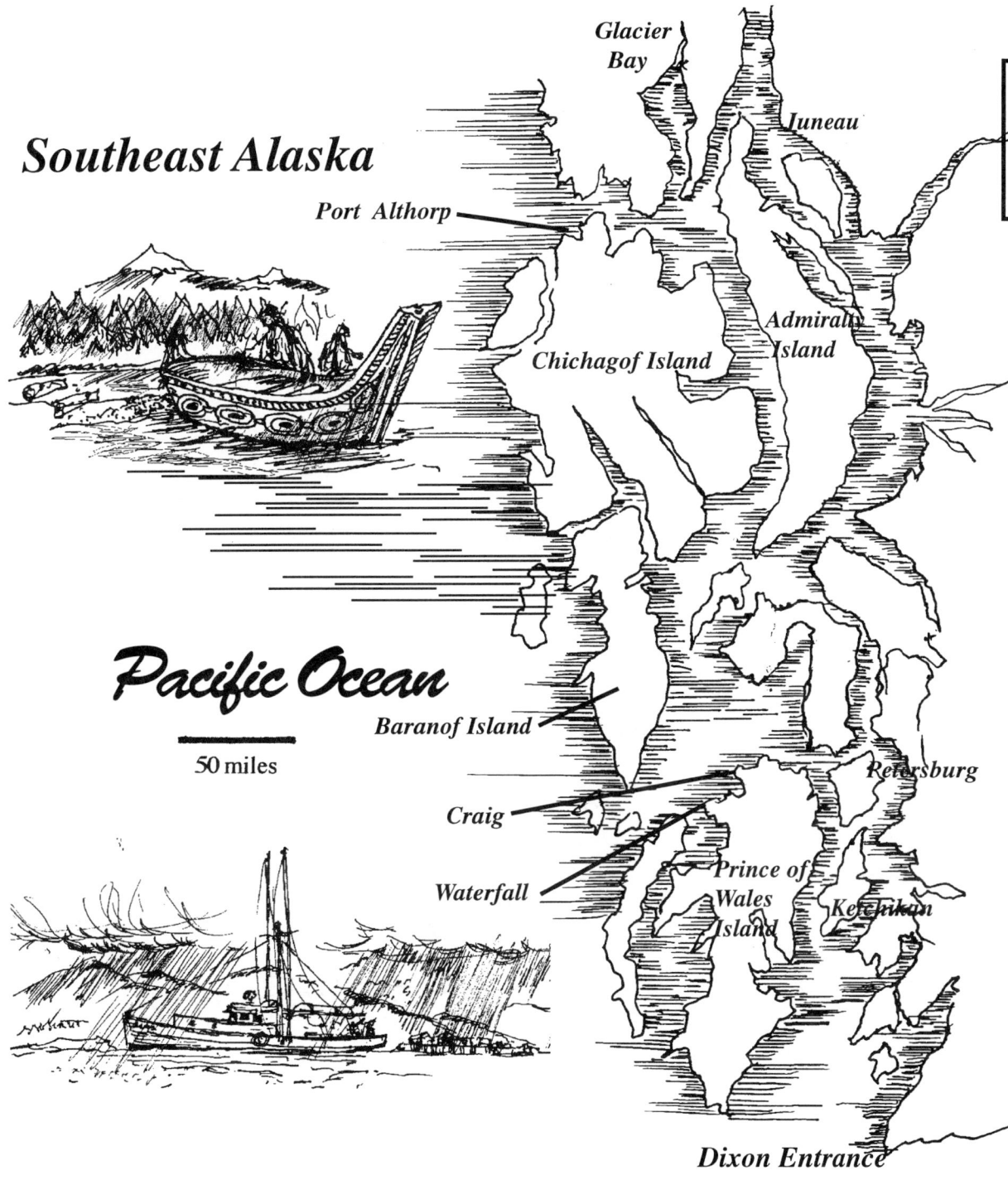

Southeast Alaska

Danger
This map not to be used for purposes of navigation.

At the time of publishing, a map was deemed essential to this story. The author conducted an extensive search for a suitable example which would show the entire territory from Glacier Bay in the north to the infamous Dixon Entrance in the south. Such a map seemed impossible to find.

Then, in an incredible stroke of good fortune, an aged beachcomber discovered the map at left, tightly rolled, and floating in a corked bottle in a kelp bed at the southern end of Chichagof Island. Obviously the map is the work of some ancient being who perhaps crossed the land bridge from Asia in some long ago millennium.

In truth the map, primitive and grossly incorrect, is the work of the author who distilled it from a chart six feet high. It seemed the only way to make it fit.

The resulting configuration, appearing at left, represents a land of such immensity and loveliness that, once seen, it is etched forever in the memory of the poet or the fool.

There is about it the gray roar of winter storms and the sunlit silence of early morning inlets. Here, in this place, the simple beauty of reality outshines the bright arena of imagination. Within the shadow of such memories, the pen and map seemed woefully inadequate and probably unneeded.

Returning

I've always felt that float plane flying was like fine poetry, good booze, or sex. It should be provided only to those old enough and bright enough to enjoy such things.

Like the face of most airplanes, the instrument panel of the De Haviland Beaver looked shabby and badly used, sort of like a telephone booth in a bad part of town. Some of the paint was peeling off in places and there were bright, shiny-smooth spots where the hands of a thousand flights had moved throttles or flaps or trim tabs. Some old compass courses, leading to God knows where, were jotted around in lead pencil—small graffiti in a tough airplane. The pilot, old like me and wordless, stared straight ahead through eyes that looked like they hadn't been awake all that long. This particular Juneau, Alaska morning was chilly and we circled on the water like a confused duck waiting for the engine to heat up to body temperature. Needles on the yellow dials jumped and jiggled, and the prop spun noisily and ineffectively a poker table's distance from the front of my face. Although this was mid-June of 1995, I'd made the same flight years before as a teenaged kid. That was in 1938 in an old Bellanca with wings that flapped like a buzzard's. When I first saw the Beaver this morning, the thing looked safe and expensive. Now, I began to wonder if it could fly.

Maybe five minutes went by, then finally satisfied and isolated by earphones, the pilot's scarred throttle hand bent forward, and the engine's complacency grew into a determined roar. After a sprint of only a couple of hundred yards across the lagoon, the Beaver shook herself, unstuck the pontoons, and rising like a swan, we arched gently away from the earth. At a kite's height and about eighty knots, we swung over what appeared to be a stand of Sitka Spruce then turned toward the west climbing one rung at a time into the gray sky of morning.

This was a journey of purpose, often dreamed of and too often postponed. Following a disastrous salmon cannery fire at Port Althorp, Alaska in 1940, my stepfather, who had served there as Superintendent, my mother, and I said good-bye to a place we really cared about. As a kid, I had spent incomparable summers there in the excitement of the salmon season, working on cannery tenders, catching fish, and loving Alaska. A part of my life and a part of our dreams went up in the smoke of the fire. At fifteen, I remember standing on the rear deck of the steamer as we left for the last time watching the charred ruins of our home until they disappeared behind the corner of Three Hill Island. Now, after fifty five years, I was coming home again.

We had left Port Althorp as three, my father, my mother and I. This time the Beaver held only me and fond memories of my parents and friends, many now gone, who had treasured the place as much as I. My dad is a distant memory now, his life warped and shortened by the plunge of an automobile off a darkened dock. Several years ago my mother left quickly, her face creased in a week by lines I'd never seen before and her body painted with that final frailty that precedes a good-bye which lasts forever. There are others who birthed this book but will not read it. Kato Schwalling my friend on the *Doris E* dying on Bataan from a Japanese machine gun bullet. Bronson taking his own life in an expensive car on a secluded Seattle beach. Norman, with whom I drank and sailed, disappearing one afternoon into the shadow of years without a word or trace, and leaving a wife and children with bitter sadness and a lifetime of unanswered questions. These were gone. It was a time now to search for that which was left.

I've always felt that float plane flying was like fine poetry, good booze, or sex. It should be provided only to those old enough and bright enough to enjoy such things. This morning, we soared along under a high, broken sky, flashing through cloud bits that whizzed past like rustling pieces of white lace. Below, the blue of sea and the green of forests, soft meadows, and small, hidden, lakes rolled by on a belt of changing wonder. Crossing Icy Straits, I looked down on broaching whales leaving white commas in a virginal, clean, and living sea...the kind of majestic sight that leaves one breathless. The *Doris* had stopped running there one afternoon half a century ago leaving us in a welter of foam, a rising wind, and a scored cylinder wall.

Pleasant Island crawls by on our right. We had a fish trap there in the old days. Then, Lemesurier Island, with Willoughby Cove shining in a small shaft of sunlight which the clouds had let sneak through. The nose drops slightly and we lose altitude crossing Point Adolphus. Dad's company had a trap there too, and the old *Eagle* had nearly foundered a mile off shore hauling too many humpback salmon in a following sea. We are lower now, racing just above the breaking waves of South Inian Pass and startling sea birds on Lavinia Point.

The pilot makes a steep bank to the left as we flash over the top of Elfin Cove and settle gently on the bright water. A few coarse-dressed people line the float as the engine slows and the prop arc shimmers in the morning brightness as it ticks into quietness. Part of the journey is finished.

It was a bumpy twenty minute boat ride from Elfin Cove, south, and into the remembrance of fifty-five years gone by. I found it difficult to talk as we ran down the bay toward the old cannery site. The past essence of the place crowded in with a hundred treasured memories. Every curving hill and mountain had remained eternally as I remembered it. Rich timber thundered up the mountain sides, thinning into slanting, highland meadows of yellow green. Above all that, granite walls freckled with white, soared even higher into the sky and shadowed the lovely fjord that was once a home to me.

Farther down on the left, the entrance to Salt Chuck Inlet was half hidden by firs as usual, and guarded by short pillars of granite as if it were somebody's castle; while to the right, a giant dished mountain standing immensely high, rose as a headstone over the exact spot where the cannery had died. June meltings of snow patches sent a filmy cascade of white down the mountain's face and into a timber stand far up the ridge, and several Bald Eagles crisscrossed in the mist which screened it all. I had recalled it this way through all the passing years, back when the story began.

Before this journey starts, it seems only reasonable that I paint some kind of picture of myself to lend credence to all that follows. The Seattle in which I grew up was a prosaic place, a town of lakes, bays, and a Puget Sound of majestic proportions. The whole of it was bathed in the certainty that if it wasn't raining at the particular moment, it damn well soon would be. Born in late October of 1924, I learned at an early age that a raincoat was a second skin and that wet feet were a constant. Both were to be tolerated and indeed welcomed if that seems possible. The blessing of my life was the family into which I was born—with one notable exception. My birth-father, an itinerant tap dancer, saxophone player, and airplane pilot heard the cry of the wild goose and left my mother and me shortly after I was born. I saw him only on rare occasions in my life. Every four or five years he would pop up, stay a few days, then disappear, usually taking more with him than he left behind. In deference to me, those responsible for my upbringing never bad-mouthed him and always welcomed him with food and a smile, if not the bourbon he fancied.

My mother and I found shelter in the home of my maternal grandparents and my mother's brother, Charles, younger than she by seventeen years. The love, affection, and stability that my mother and I found with my grandparents and my uncle transcended the ordinary because they were very extraordinary people. If I am anything of value, much of the credit must go to my grandmother and grandfather, whose love and direction turned a sow's ear into something faintly resembling a silk purse.

My grandmother was just over six feet tall which was an incredible height for a woman of her era. A former school teacher in frontier Montana, she was a woman of indomitable will and limitless compassion. I learned a lot of life's lessons while I dried dishes beside her. When I was in the first grade, she caught me both stealing and lying in the same day. Her words at my bedtime were few and everlasting: a two minute treatise on what was right and what was wrong. I never stole or lied to her again. Simply said, she was the paragon of what all people should be. I believed it as a child. Seventy years of living have not changed my opinion.

Charlie Rehm, my grandfather, was a man of enduring courage. In the last decade of the 1800's, he came west on the rods of a freight car. With a cheap horse and a good rifle he rode the rough parts of south-central Montana not long after the "mischief" at the Little Big Horn. For six months, he searched for a spot of his own and finally homesteaded on the Crow Indian Reservation just a tad before they were ready to leave. His immense hands, dark brown and callused had sheared sheep and broken horses. The same hands now fed and sheltered us and gentled me as a child. My Grandparents have been gone for many years, but nearly every day the debt of love I owe them gets installment payments of remembrance.

My mother was stronger than she thought she was, but she was not born with the will and the strength of her mother and father. She was rather slight and verging on the delicate. There were many long days of illness for her during my younger years. She was born in a cattle line-shack in Montana in 1903, but she was more ballet than frontier. Early on she aspired to a dance career, but that didn't happen. I suspect the reason for that non-achievement wasn't circumstances so much as a lack of the determination necessary to make the dream come true. In the really difficult days of the thirties when everyone had to contribute she tried to pull her share of the wagon for both of us. Oft times she couldn't do that. There were bouts of pleurisy and a rather short lived nervous breakdown that mystified and worried me as a child. Some of my earliest memories are of my mother lying in a darkened room and my grandmother saying I should be quiet and not bother her because she was sick. The important things she gave me were a lifetime of caring and an unshakable faith in the things I could do—that is a gift of value.

Charles, my uncle, was like a brother to me. He was the type of kid everyone would want to have. Bright, industrious, and achieving, he was the kite and I was the tail. That type of situation is never totally satisfying to the underling, but I had no trouble dealing with it because of my love and respect for him. Charles always knew where he was going. He had developed his life plan in the crib. As expected, he ended up as a respected and loved physician in Seattle and has enjoyed a lifetime crowned with success.

These then are four of the people who cast me and freed me slowly from the mold.

We lived in a large two-story house where a lot of love abounded and the lawn was seldom cut. Later on there was a fifth, my stepfather. I will speak of him in the pages ahead. Whatever the season, I shared a life and a living space with people who cared for me and what I was to become. It was a rich and beautiful place in which to grow.

Growing

It was a breath and almost a presence of docks, wet oilskins, sailors, rope, nets, fish, creosote and diesel oil.

I believe people are born with certain sleeping passions. As I think about it, they might be better described as "connectors" by which people plug into their world and into life. As the individual grows and develops, these connections light up and burst into patterns of interest and life styles which remain forever fixed and unchanged. I have always loved boats and if there were ever boats and a sea to love, they were around me as a child. The Seattle of my youth was all boats. Large, patrician vessels, equipped with bright flags and stemware martini glasses, crisscrossed the waters of wealthy Lake Washington; and all types of working craft plied Puget Sound, smacking of far off places and limitless adventure. Huge sailing barkentines lined the shores of Lake Union resting between voyages to Alaska and the fishing grounds. The barkentines moored there were square rigged with tall masts encased in spider webs of manila line that had purpose, but were too complex for me to understand. These ships were the quintessence of adventure and I see them still in wonder through the eyes of my childhood. They lined the shores, leaning against massive piers and wharves, dying by inches as the years went by. As I grew, one by one they disappeared, and by the time I started looking at girls, these ships and their era had vanished forever into the fog of the past..

It was only natural that the Pacific Northwest would be oriented to the sea. Everywhere one looked there was water. Even in hard times kids learned to sail early. High school kids built and raced their own "flatties," a sixteen foot centerboard sail boat. If their families had money, they moved on to bigger and faster boats. The city was dotted with yacht clubs and immersed in marine repair and storage facilities. Salmon fishing in Puget Sound was excellent, and thousands of families owned fishing skiffs or rowboats The University of Washington was a true giant in the sport of shell racing, and George Pocock, the premier builder of racing shells, supplied his beautiful craft to racing fraternities all over the world. The Ballard locks was a "must-see" for visitors. Around the clock, boats of all shapes and sizes climbed up or down the water staircase that led from Lake Washington and Lake Union to Puget Sound and ultimately to the North Pacific. The suburb of Ballard was an ethnic enclave of Swedes and Norwegians whose ancestors had sailed the waters of the world. They brought with them their kinship to the sea, and their work boats and fishing craft constituted a major part of the Seattle scene.

To satisfy my lust for all things marine, my mother and I occasionally took trips to nearby places on ferries of the old Black Ball Lines. By the age of six or seven, I had learned to treasure the sound of surrounding fog horns and to listen, with pleasure, to the rhythm and constant shudder of the slow speed diesels that pushed us along. I particularly loved the old tug boats that were moored close to Colman Dock in downtown Seattle. They were painted with rich, glossy, reds and blacks looking tough and majestic with hulls thick enough to last the ages. There was a nobility about them as they nodded fore and aft and rested with dignity in the dirty wharf water around them. A slight plume of mist usually rose from the stacks of the old steam rigs; a warm boiler made for faster starts and the tow boat business was very competitive in those days. The tugboat which first arrived on the scene usually got the tow.

Some of the old boats had changed their overalls by replacing ancient steam engines with the newer diesels. Steam or diesel, their power plants were immense and primitive, dwarfing the men that served them. Like neighborhood bullies, these vessels were born to push things around. Old rubber tires lined their rub rails to cushion the shock of constant contact with ships fifty-times their size. Usually, for direct confrontation, they had a huge, thick, pad like a manila Band-Aid on their bow. Many of them carried the Foss Family name and there were others whose names spoke of strength and the sea like *Neptune* and *Hercules*.

Often before I went to sleep, I pictured myself as skipper on a towboat. With one hand on the wheel and my head out the lowered window, I would shout orders to a deck gang while we pushed a loaded barkentine toward the open sea. I never missed a *Tugboat Annie* movie. I particularly recall the one in which Wallace Beery had to crawl into a hot steam boiler to make repairs. He saved the day and the tugboat, and emerged into the waiting arms of a gruffly grateful and adoring Marie Dressler. The setting for those stories was the town of *Secoma*, whose name was merely a joining of the names of Tacoma and my hometown of Seattle.

Besides the ferries and the movies there was, of course, my grandfather and "the Market." We still held hands crossing the street when my grandfather first took me to a place of wonders called the Pike Place Market. It was, in my opinion, simply the best place in the world from which to see the water craft which constantly crossed the waters of the Sound. Perched beneath a ramshackle roof on a hill above the waterfront were countless stalls where one could buy anything to eat, drink, or wear. We went there quite often during the depression buying what seemed essential and merely looking at that which was not. It was and is Seattle's timeless treasure, an engrossing place filled with the shouts of fish mongers, curio sellers, jostling tourists and single minded locals. Everybody there was looking for a bargain. Amidst the frenzied commerce, even the hookers had discount sales.

Over the market, like the icing on a birthday cake, the prevailing westerly brought the multifaceted smell of the sea. Its breath brought a presence of docks, wet oilskins, sailors, rope, nets, fish, creosote and diesel oil. For me it was an irresistible incense, as much a part of the place as the sights and sounds that I still recall and savor after sixty-five years. Between the vendors' stalls, I could look west through the filthy windows and see vessels of all types leaving their paw prints on the Sound, pockmarked with the ever falling rain. Through good luck and chance, I've seen the great Harbors of the world: Hong Kong, the Malabar Coast of India, New York Harbor, Truk Lagoon, Alexandria, London Docks, Shanghai and maybe a hundred more. But the view of Puget Sound through the dirty windows of the Pike Place Market was filled with all the color and excitement that a kid could want. It was a lasting treasure, one of many which have filled my years.

The great stock market crash of 1929 occurred within days of my fifth birthday. The people of America were about to be pounded flat on an anvil of poverty and heartbreak. It would be soon in the coming. Hardship crept across the nation like a bad smell. Without a moment's outburst of anger or anguish, my grandfather and grandmother saw the loss of all for which they had worked so hard. With millions of others, the five of us walked into a time of want. As a child, I was spared the worst of it by the sacrifices readily made by those around me. There was a great and tragic sameness among people in the desperate years of the early 30's, and the pattern of our family matched the melancholy of millions of others. We lost our home through foreclosure to a lousy mortgage company while everyone in the family was working in the drive to survive. New shoes were a cause for celebration and, like nearly everybody else, we owed money at the neighborhood grocery store.

Sometimes we did get new stuff. I remember the time my mother bought me a real leather coat with a sheep skin collar. We rode downtown on the old # 21 Seattle streetcar that wiggled and shook its way through Phinney Ridge and past Woodland Park. It eventually disgorged us on downtown Third Avenue. After a walk of a block or two, my mother, with little money and mountains of determination, entered the clothing establishment of Browning, King & Company while I followed dutifully behind. It was a nice store which we seldom visited in the depression years.

She was a pretty bright and a good looking 30 year old with a great figure. She also had a full appreciation of the tough dollars she earned working in a dismal part of town for a skinflint credit company. When she bought her kid a coat, she was sure as hell going to get her money's worth! I've forgotten the cost of the coat and that's unimportant. The fact was, my mother drove a hard bargain and did very well indeed. We left the establishment with two shopping bags containing the coat, a large box of magic tricks labeled *CHANDU THE MAGICIAN,* a black beanie hat, two balsa gliders, a couple pairs of knee length socks and a huge kit model of the H.M.S. *Bounty*. The fact that the middle-aged salesman liked her looks probably had something to do with it.

Like any poor kid I held tightly to the *Bounty* model going home on the street car. A toy was a precious thing in the thirties. I remember there was a picture of the ship in full color on the shiny top of the box. I knew it was going to open a new world for me. The kit had masts and spars and a lot of little brass cannons and brass portholes. Even the glue was included. It was a great day for me, but a bad day for the clothing salesman. After the sale, he asked my mother for a date and she turned him down. I believe she mumbled something like "too old and too fat," after we'd left the store and were walking back to the streetcar.

I don't know how long I labored on the *Bounty*. It was a long time for a kid who always worked in a frenzy. When I glued the last piece and tied the last knot, I was very proud of it. It was a pretty decent job, painted black above and green below the waterline. I used to push it very slowly across the seamy living room carpet, as if I were entering some strange and exotic harbor for the first time. We dodged rocks and other dangers and anchored at last in a place of peace and beauty in the corner of the room. I feel the same things today when I sail a twenty-five foot gaff rigged Monterey sail boat that is so lovely people stare at it. There's a good argument for the possibility that I've never really grown up.

For a couple of years, I periodically sailed the *Bounty* over the seven seas between the ugly chesterfield and the legs of the dining room table. I cruised my own world and made believe the carpet was a sea that went on forever. I had a make-believe first mate whom I named Bill Cargo. We always sailed together, riding the monstrous waves in mid-carpet and nestling into snug harbors around the edges of the room. To hell with baseball and kick the can. If a guy had a boat, there was a whole world to explore. Bill Cargo and I explored it together, shipmates to the end.

Then somewhere one day my model of the *Bounty* sailed out of reach and out of sight of the kid who was growing within me. The carpet was no longer a raging sea, it was just something to walk on and the snug harbors at the corners of the living room vanished with the passing times and became merely places that were hard to vacuum. I think the *Bounty* ended up in the garbage can, but she lies safely anchored on a small bay of memories in my past, moored alongside the *Doris E*, a beautiful, gutsy Alaskan tug boat that was destined to be a big part of my future.

Meanwhile, the overture of my life continued in a sheltered way. My family worked hard to protect me from the reality outside our doors. My grandfather took menial carpentry jobs and Charles worked for a butter and egg man close to the Pike Place Market. My mother was doing better and took a job with KJR/KOMO, a local radio station. My grandmother held the reins and kept the wagon going while I did a lot of dishes and took out the garbage. And there were a lot of other important commitments like making my bed, turning on the water heater, keeping the furnace going, and not forgetting to say, "Now I lay me down," etc. These tasks were assigned and monitored by my grandparents with ultimate patience and ultimate love. My mother, working full time, never neglected to provide the affection a kid requires and Charles tried to help me with my homework. In the meantime, I was growing taller, a little wiser, and dragging myself to John B. Allen grade school where I shone as a notable underachiever.

I really didn't hate school; it was just that I thought there were better ways to spend time, even on rainy days. As in other areas, my academic achievements were totally eclipsed by my Uncle Charles, a brilliant, straight "A" student who soared through the grades like an eagle. In retrospect, unlike Charles, I spent a lot of time staring out of schoolroom windows, drawing pictures of boats and airplanes and writing poems that I didn't let other people see. I was part of the great "unwashed" who didn't perform well in the classroom arena. I was no problem to teachers. I was a neutral entity who, unknown to the authorities, was hearing and soaking up quite a bit of miscellaneous learning. One day I decided to throw off the bounds of mediocrity. We had been studying poetry and I astounded the teacher by asking if I might recite Longfellow's *Hiawatha*. I didn't mean part of it, I meant the whole thing. I'd memorized it at home because it was something I liked and I wanted to have it with me to think about from time to time. At the finish of my recitation, there was a sweet moment of total silence that I still savor. The teacher looked at me strangely for a little while. It was as if she'd missed something. She had missed something, I wasn't as dumb as I looked. But, after a week, Longfellow fell by the wayside and I went back to window watching, dreaming about boats and the sea, and having trouble with twelve times twelve.

Changes

H.V.V. Bean taught me about astrolabes, chronometers and the sextant. He showed me how to eye-splice and explained that those things used to tie up boats were not ropes but lines.

It was September in 1936 that my mother went to work for the Skinner and Eddy Corporation, an organization of some power and prestige in Seattle. They had interests in logging, shipbuilding and timber as well as being the parent company for the Alaska Pacific Salmon Company. The latter was to have a dramatic effect on my future and the ever present pursuit of my interest in boats, Alaska, and the sea. I remember her coming home one day and remarking about the sorrow she felt for a man who had just lost his wife to cancer. It was the first time I had ever heard the name Oscar Larson, the man who was to become my stepfather. The Alaska Pacific Salmon Company employed him as Superintendent of a cannery at a place called Port Althorp in Southeastern Alaska. I looked it up and read about it. The cannery was located on Chichagof Island, a haven for tall trees and huge brown bears. I recall mouthing the word "Oscar" several times and chuckling at the fact that it was really kind of a ridiculous name. After a decent length of time, Oscar Larson began seeing my mother on a fairly regular basis. His interest and love was the best thing that ever happened to my mother and me.

I had been fatherless for twelve years, and it was a deprivation that had become an ongoing, somewhat depressing reality. I got plenty of love at home, but something was missing. I found myself wondering how it would be to have a father who lived in. My birth-father crossed the threshold only infrequently, smiling, joking, and leaving. If the need for a father image hadn't been important to me then, I wouldn't remember it now. In one depression-era elementary classroom, I was the only child with divorced parents. I remember that as being hurtful and embarrassing. The disclosure of my status was prompted by a stupid question directed by an unthinking teacher. I've never forgotten it.

As my mother and Oscar Larson began to see each other more often, I discovered a strong association beginning to build between us. He made a threesome out of the relationship. We went to boxing matches, football, and basketball games and he taught me how to bowl. I spent a lot of time with him at the rather exclusive Washington Athletic Club, quite often without my mother. At his side, I learned some Norwegian cuss words and some funny little songs that I now sing to my grandchildren. The relationship was easy and it wasn't long before I began to cherish the time he spent with me.

It's difficult to understand how he became an effective parent-figure given the structure of his early years. He was born in 1890 on a small farm outside the tiny town of Harmony, Minnesota, and came from a devout Norwegian family with a dour outlook on life and a religious rigidity as hard as steel. As far as I could tell, most members of his family never learned how to smile. I remember a brown-tone photograph of the clan grouped in front of a modest, unexciting, bungalow. With the exception of my stepfather and his sister, Nettie, the family's faces are cast in an eternal melancholy. Even the dog seems forlorn.

In 1909, the Larson family moved from Minnesota to Parkland, Washington, a dull suburb of Tacoma. Oscar Larson went first to Alaska in the spring of 1910, working for the Northwestern Fisheries Company at a cannery site located at Boca de Quadra southeast of a small frontier-like town called Ketchikan. The Buschmann family, Alaska pioneers, originally owned the cannery, and it is highly probable that Oscar got the job through his sister's romantic association with August Buschmann whom she would marry.

Oscar was an exacting man who demanded much of himself and of those who worked with and for him. There was little of the exciting or unexpected in his work habits and his attention to detail and a penchant for keeping records made him ideally suited to serve as bookkeeper or superintendent of a salmon cannery.

Alaskan salmon canneries were, in fact, small, primitive towns far removed from the rest of society. They required a total degree of self-sufficiency and the superintendent and bookkeeper headed up a defacto ruling hierarchy serving as king and prince, judge, jury and executioner. The twenty-four hour per day management jobs were complex and demanding; there was literally no time during the canning season when management was off the job. To further complicate the situation, operation of the canneries required the combined efforts of several ethnic groups. Caucasians filled those jobs dealing with management and mid-management responsibilities, which included mechanics, carpenters, boat skippers and boat crews, storekeepers, fish trap builders and others involved with the technology of the time. Chinese or Filipino workers dealt with the process of canning and actually made salmon cans on site in the early days. They also engaged in operating canning machinery and performing such other repetitive canning tasks as were required. Native Americans, the majority of whom were from the Tlingit group, operated their own fishing boats while the Native women performed various tasks in the canning process.

Each year, these disparate ethnic mixtures and language groups were assembled and transported to an isolated and hostile environment almost totally devoid of any recreational pursuits. They worked long hours in close proximity to each other. The presence of foremen who oversaw the activities of their own groups eased the tensions somewhat, but the situation was fraught with danger. Though carefully watched, the trigger of illicit booze sometimes trickled in from passing fishing boats. It was the kind of thing that could cause trouble. In short, the canning season was always a pot on the back burner waiting to boil over. Amazingly, and to the everlasting credit of all concerned, it never did.

I have spoken at length about my stepfather because he was the intrinsic link that bound my mother and me to a new life. He was everything my birth-father had never been. It was during late July of 1938 that my mother told me she intended to marry him. The prospect delighted me. He had been kind and understanding to a thirteen year old who needed direction and, by that time, had become a part of my life. The stories he told me about Alaska were endless and fascinating to a kid looking for new adventures. What also interested me was the fact that his responsibilities as Superintendent of the salmon cannery also included responsibility for the Company's fleet of cannery tenders. For me, there was an inherent romance and charisma to these boats. Tough, strong and colorful, they were first cousins to the tugs which lined Seattle's waterfront. I memorized their names before I ever saw them: *Doris E, Sally S, Lloyd C, Service, Hero, and Eagle*, and Oscar described them in minute detail. A short time later, my mother told me that we would leave for Alaska in August and meet Oscar in Juneau. Following their marriage we were to go to the cannery at Port Althorp and stay there for several weeks while the cannery was being closed down for the winter. It was all I had hoped for.

Another experience concerning boats and Alaska was also about to impact my life. Friends of my grandparents maintained a cabin in Southworth, a small community across Puget Sound from Seattle. We occasionally visited them, staying for several days at a time. During the summer of 1938, my Mother accepted an invitation for us to stay for two weeks prior to our journey to Alaska. It was a delightful place filled with a prewar peace and open spaces made for a teenage kid. On the second day of our Southworth stay I made the acquaintance of Mr. H.V.V. Bean a local octogenarian, and a man whom I would quickly grow to love and admire,. The double V's are no mistake. English born and bred, he insisted on their usage. He was a person whose kinship with the sea was like something out of *Treasure Island* and the difference in our ages bound us even closer than had we been contemporaries.

Through some fortuitous set of circumstances, Mr. H.V.V. Bean had spent years in Alaska. He had crewed on sailing ships visiting many of the places I would soon see. He was thin and tall with a quiet but authoritative voice which, while brooking no nonsense, could also soften and touch the imagination of a teenage boy. He was properly bearded as any real mariner must be and, in him, I saw the embodiment of the men who sailed the *Hispaniola* and the *Bounty* hull-down into the lands of adventure and danger which I had read about in books. I remember his face as being chiseled in a lean and wrinkle-less pattern with eyes that sought contact and response. We shared days filled with sun, rain and the clear, cold waters of a rocky shore an arm's length from his front porch. Age and youth, a shared respect, and the leisure time to see the worth in each other combined to fill those days with the joy of new visions and discovery. We were two kites tethered on a single string sharing interests and stories that were close to a lifetime apart.

Before we had met, he had built a large skiff from heavy cedar planks with the intention of fishing for cod. There was good fishing on tide changes that washed the channel between his beach and Vashon Island, a stone's throw away. The skiff, brown-red and shining, rested on a covered porch close to the lapping waters of the Sound. She carried polished brass oarlocks and a brass ring in the bow. A line of honest, three-strand manila was spliced through the bow ring for mooring. We talked often of taking her out for a row but because of our years, his too many and mine too few, neither of us could budge her from her appointed resting place. We chose to sit near her though when he taught me some of the knowledge his years at sea had given him. It was as though the skiff was a kind of symbol; a confirmation of what he once was and what I wanted to be.

H.V.V. Bean taught me about astrolabes, chronometers, and the sextant. He showed me how to eye-splice and explained that those things used to tie up boats were not ropes but lines. His collection of charts showed pictures of the Alaska I would get to know first hand. They were old, yellow and so tightly rolled they crackled and fought the unrolling. We treated them with the deference and care accorded the *Dead Sea Scrolls*. With the four corners held down with books and a small, ancient compass of devious dependability we explored together the whole of Southeastern Alaska. We covered everything: channels, islands, rocks, and reefs. After a navigation lesson, we would release the charts from their temporary bondage and they would roll themselves back up like yellowed window blinds. The ancient mariner would then return them to our Ark of The Covenant, an old pine foot locker with a bronze hasp and lock. In all likelihood after our last look, H.V.V. Bean probably never removed them again. Like a lot of things we shared, the charts were only small joys to remember. Years later, I suppose they went begging in a garage sale somewhere. People probably haggled over whether they were worth a dime or a quarter a piece. To me, each yellowed sheet was a portrait of adventure telling me where I would soon be going. I longed for the journey to begin.

And, that summer, there was time for me to be alone in an idyllic setting, tailor-made for a thirteen year old. The whole of the region held the spirit of land close to a great sea. Southworth was very like an island. It was isolated and set apart, gleaming in the gin-clear waters of the Sound. The days were mine to use as I saw fit with little responsibility and the opportunity for constant homemade adventuring. The farm-like houses were old and sparse and the country was alive with meadows cradling fresh water ponds especially made for bent-pin fishing. There was a New England feeling about Southworth, an aging beyond its years. It was as if someone had put it there and then had walked off and blissfully forgotten about it. The beaches were rocky and held endless treasures of small marine skeletons; Japanese glass fishing floats, bright colored rocks, polished bits of soft-edged glass and other items that I could use to fill my pockets. A beach walk was a daily ritual which I never neglected.

A lifetime of periodic introspection has enabled me to learn quite a bit about myself. I take a small measure of pride in being sensitive to things and people around me. At times, the level of my sensitivity has caused me some trouble and some pain, but I don't think I'd want to give it up for an equal measure of anything else. There is a by-product of this condition. On rare occasion, reality and imagination have pressed together so closely upon me they have forever embossed moments of my life with personal highs and transcending insights which I really value. The memory of these instances is intense and lasts a lifetime; one happened during the ending days of my Southworth summer.

I had spent the afternoon walking on the beach looking for the rocks, glass and debris that served me as pocket fillers. Weather wise the day was decent enough, sort of average with a watery sun but enough warmth to be comfortable. Close to sunset on a beach a mile or more from home, I came upon the dead body of a small shark with a baby protruding from the birth canal. I examined it rather carefully wondering for a little time about the nature of death. I'm sure most kids think about that. There was no concern or worry. It was just in the nature of a curiosity about the fates that decided that some things live and some things die. I walked on hoping to find some glass floats.

I recall sitting for a time on a rather large cedar log looking toward the Northeast and Blake Island a mile away. Blake was a smallish island, heavily wooded, and privately owned. It was well patrolled and a place upon which trespassing was strictly forbidden. Southworth residents spoke softly and suspiciously of the isolation of the island, spicing the talk with little hints of the occult. I was aware of the forbidding nature of the place, wondering at times about what secrets or mysteries might be abroad there.

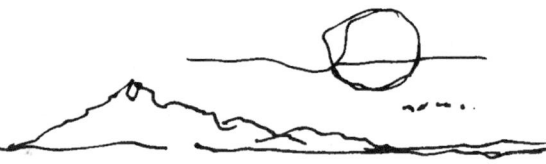

With the sun falling below the hills behind me, the fading light turned the channel and the island into a metallic blue-purple. An incoming fog began to crawl down the passage blurring images and erasing details that belonged to the light of day. With the coming darkness, a remarkable personal stillness slowly descended upon my mind and the scene I was watching. I became aware of a joining of vision, thought, and hearing that was acute and magical. The experience was incredible. I feared that even turning my head might destroy the instant. All senses and sights had joined in an awareness that transcended reality. Color, sound, feel, time, the movement of far gulls and even the pervasive silence had assumed a surrealistic, dreamlike quality that was at once forbidding and enticing. I sensed there was something bright just beyond the edge of the experience. I tried to "think" myself towards it but it was something that I could not reach or touch or understand. The occurrence was unique and a little frightening. Then, the extraordinary minutes left as surely and slowly as they had arrived. A memory of sixty years is the only proof of their existence.

I walked home in the darkness, humbled by the experience and wondering if there was something wrong with me. It crossed my mind that the whole thing might have been a product of my conjecture about death and the small shark and its baby. One thing was certain. For some small time there had been a transformation, a change in my being, another state of awareness and acuity. I had ventured ever so close to a vividness and reality I had never known before. It concerned me for some time afterward until I realized that something special had occurred out there on the beach, something that was beyond my immediate need to understand and to share. It would fit easily into a special pocket along with the rocks and polished glass I collected, and the memory of my dear friend H.V.V. Bean. It had been quite a summer vacation.

The S.S. *North Sea*

Flagship of the Northland Transportation Company, she was built in 1918 as a freighter and christened the *Admiral Peoples*. In 1924 she was converted to a passenger vessel and cruised Caribbean waters. In 1934, renamed, she began service to Alaska under the Northland Transportation flag. On February 14, 1947, while southbound from Alaska, she struck a rock in Seaforth channel near Bella Bella, British Columbia. Efforts to save her proved futile. Years later she was salvaged as scrap. She was a fine vessel, well found and dearly loved by the author.

Journey

This was different from a ride on the ferry. I was heading for a place far beyond the reaches of Puget Sound and beyond the reaches of the islands and passages that I could see out ahead of me.

The day of our leaving for Alaska was packed with such excitement I can recall it with ease. Oscar had booked passage for us to travel to Alaska on the Northland Transportation Company's flag ship, the *SS North Sea*. She was built in 1918 as a freighter and christened the *Admiral Peoples*. In 1924, the year I was born, she was converted to a passenger ship, serving the Florida and Caribbean trade. Ten years later, in 1934 she began service to Alaska. The *North Sea* was not huge, but she was large enough to provide a hundred nooks and crannies for a kid to explore. One great feature was a well-deck forward from which I could watch porpoises darting back and forth across our bow wave. For the few years that lay ahead for us both, the *North Sea* was special to me. During the five days we were en route to Juneau, I got to know the ship and the people that made it go. There was a real joy in surveying every inch of the vessel from the shaft alley to the wheel house. It was all new and virgin territory to a kid who liked boats.

Northland Transportation ships departed from the Northland Company Pier in downtown Seattle. It was one of many huge docking facilities slanting at an angle from the shore into the gray-green waters of the sound. Huge painted letters identified the owners of each mammoth structure, and generations of noisome gulls had carelessly painted their roofs chalk-white. The piers fronted on a broad no-nonsense thoroughfare aptly named Alaskan Way. The broad street was chaotic and was usually filled with trucks which were either double parked or anxiously honking their way from one spot to another. There was a fascinating intensity to everything that happened there.

On the day we left, my grandparents delivered us to the dock in style. On the way downtown my grandfather gripped the wheel of his 1935 Hudson Terraplane automobile as if it were a set of reins. That was nothing new. His time straddled the horse-automobile era. He was from a generation who often forgot themselves and said "Whoa" to cars. The old Hudson served him on his job sites and was in truth half car and half truck. For this auspicious occasion, the rear interior had been temporarily swept clear of nails, plaster and other debris. My mother and I rode in style seated on a tattered blue plush seat that shortly before had been a repository for hammers and saws. It was the kind of a car seat that required that you dust yourself off after you got out to keep your rear end free of plaster dust and shavings. My grandfather liked to tie stuff on top of the car like boards and long ladders. Quite often, after the untying, the ropes remained attached to the automobile. This situation created a lot of confusion for following traffic, and it often appeared as if the old Terraplane were running away after breaking its leash. On this day all ropes had been removed and we traveled in at least a semblance of dignity and respectability.

When we arrived at the cavernous dock, there was something of bedlam about the scene. People scurried everywhere while stinking little gasoline-engine tractors towed carts loaded with boxes across the pier's rough timbered floor. Longshoremen with huge arms and dirty shirts guided pallets aboard the ship, loading the last of the northbound freight. Everywhere there was action and noise and above it all hung the heavy essence of creosote and salt water, the "body smell" of docks and the sea. After we had checked our luggage and climbed the gangplank, I looked back to watch a gaggle of people corralled

like sheep behind a white picket fence. They were the ones who stayed behind. In the gloom of the dock's shingle roof, those who were staying stood awkwardly or shifted from one anxious foot to another and waited to smile or cry a particular brand of good-bye. There was an awkwardness about them like guests with slow farewells who don't know whether to go or stay and thus linger too long at the open front door.

My grandparents stood in the crowd, and I recall the intensity of my grandmother's eyes as a loud and welcomed whistle announced our imminent departure. She had been my mother for nearly fourteen years. She and her husband had written the script for what I had become. They had loved the poor student and loved the demanding, emotional, offender who early on had used crayons on the stipple-plastered wall in their living room. Then, later in depression times, the same kid had broken their costly front window with a badly thrown baseball. Now he was going away to live with someone else. My grandfather didn't wave much, but I could see he watched me for a long time. If my grandmother cried she waited until we were gone. They were selfless then, as they had been selfless through all the heavy years.

Someone gave me a wax paper package of rolls of confetti, perhaps a dozen bright narrow rings of colored paper. When thrown to those on the dock, they formed a last tender bond between those going and those staying behind. There were a few friends there to see us go, but I tossed most of my confetti to my grandmother and grandfather. As the ship slid slowly astern, hundreds of the colored paper ribbons parted and flickered brightly in the wind against the brilliant white side of the *North Sea*. I'd like to think that those connecting my grandmother, my grandfather, and me were the last ones to break.

There was a new life beginning with this journey. As the ship stood out in the channel it was easy to spot the dingy windows lining the waterfront side of the Pike Place Market. I had stared through them so often from the vendors' stalls wondering where the paths of my seas might lead. There was a symbolism about seeing the windows now from another direction and finding a whole new world of adventure to enjoy. I had a new vision that was running hard to catch up with the arc of dreams that lay ahead of me. I thought about that a little bit while I was standing at the rail. Then I started looking for a way to get down to the engine room.

With a smart wind blowing down-channel, the *North Sea* shuddered gently as the bridge turned the engine telegraph from astern to slow ahead. She swung easily to port then picked up speed and headed north out of Elliot Bay. Our stateroom was on the starboard side and I recall watching the dun colored hills of the mainland swing across the port hole on an endless belt of miles and time. Within hours we were abeam Port Townsend and, in a slight swell, we sidestepped our way past The San Juan and Gulf Islands. There was always a retinue of hovering gulls seeking anything even remotely edible. I don't remember, but if things were as they should be, there were probably low clouds about with a hint of rain to come. I had removed myself from my mother at an early instant wishing to project the image of a seasoned traveler and bon-vivant. After extensive exploration, I found a place of shelter on the fantail. The aft deck house protected it from the wind, and it would be my special place for the remainder of the voyage. With a turned-up coat collar and an itchy wool watch cap, I sat on a huge cleat of black iron enjoying an orchestra seat to the constantly changing visual immensity around me. There was nothing static, nothing was still. The ship lived with the pulse of the turning screw while an endlessly changing pattern of white and green wake rolled out astern to vanish in the blue grayness two hundred yards behind us. I listened to the sound of wind and felt the subliminal vibrations and jiggling that whisper of movement and passage. This was different from a ride on the ferry. I was heading for a place far beyond the scope of Puget Sound and beyond the reaches of the islands and passages that I could see out ahead of me. Days and nights would pass before I arrived. The chart I had purchased at Lowman and Hanford was stretched out on my bunk below. I had marked it with the courses Mr. H.V.V Bean and I had laid out. I knew where I was going, and there was an excitement to it that made me draw in my breath and let it out very slowly.

Too soon, I was called in to an early dinner after a desperate search by my Mother who was afraid I had stumbled overboard. She would get over that. We sat in a far corner in the Dining Salon in seats reserved for the less esteemed. I fidgeted through the mysteries of a menu in French that required considerable direction and explanation. Such pretense did not come easily to a kid from Phinney Ridge who thought everybody used an oilcloth table cover. I had always favored pretty plain fare like hot dogs and Campbell's Tomato Soup. Here, I was faced with items on a menu the names of which were totally incomprehensible. The distinct probability existed that the stuff wouldn't taste all that good either, and I always had to clean up my plate. I didn't spend a great deal of time in the dining room, it was a little like church, confining and not much fun. Early experiences like this have created a lifetime aversion to menus written in French. I still don't like or understand them and have never learned to savor the exotic foods they represent.

Following dinner, I returned to my perch on the fantail. The timing was perfect. Coming darkness began to erase the color of the world and birthed dark outlines and a new universe filled with sparkling pin points of light stretching out to me from a shore that was slowly but surely moving away. An occasional stab of double brilliance told of the headlights of a car inadvertently and momentarily aimed toward us from a curving road. Now and again, a dash of bright color betrayed a shore-bound intersection of something, somewhere, not really worthy of analysis.

And, there were other night time lights of which H.V.V. Bean had spoken...lights that sing out of the blackness directing our pathway and speaking of the romance of where we were. A passing towboat shows a port running light and triple whites on the masthead. The combination whispers the warning of a tow far astern. Off the bow ahead, a seiner or trolling boat turns and changes color red to green like some seagoing chameleon, then heads for a dimly lit somewhere in the surrounding black. Rather close aboard, a red lighted bell buoy winks and slow-dances alongside in the ripple of our passing wake...its heavy bell-clapper swings to drop a brutish clanking in the pool of night. Rustled from sleep and having had its truculent say, the buoy moves astern ceasing to speak to us until we pass this way again. There is a theater of vessels here, orbiting, passing, crossing, and recrossing in a voiceless light-choreographed ballet. They avoid collision by changing the color of their eyes and they speak the nature of their form and shape in a language of dim lamps the system has prescribed. The waltzing arches back and forth across the black waters of the channel as far as the eye can see; but there are limits. The voyagers are contained and regulated by far pinpoints of flashing brilliance and by buoys, bells, whistles, and throaty diaphones, all of them setting the rhythm and the beat. They must be carefully observed, and each must be obeyed without question. These lights and sounds are the "Lords of the Dance," choreographing the participants as they move across the night-sea. At a late hour, the cold wind across the deck drives me inside to a warm bed. Sixty years have not dimmed the wonders of this day and night nor the joy in the retelling. Sometime after midnight, we pass Gabriola Reef heading northeast up the Strait of Georgia. By that time the callow navigator is fast asleep.

In retirement now and, with that special joy reserved for the elderly, I sail a small boat, well found and well equipped. Though its sail plan is ancient, and its hull design goes back to the Mediterranean cradle of man, the navigation instruments I carry are small miracles. They make me the Master Mariner I am not. Since I have the money to buy these wonder toys they keep me well informed and replace the senses I should rely upon. Their dials and numbers shout in my ear telling me where I am, where I am bound, and how long it will take me to get there. Another small box writes notes telling me of the depth and temperature of the water beneath my keel and even if there are fish about. I have a radio to call others at sea or ashore or to declare some type of emergency should one suddenly occur. Through fog or dark of night one more small box with a peep hole in it penetrates the veil and draws me a picture of everything about me. I am a highly qualified Master of the Sea. I am an explorer like Magellan, Columbus, Nelson, Drake and all of the others. I am all these things. Then, somewhere in the system a tiny switch fails, and I am reduced to a small, blind creature in a tiny boat on a sea too large to comprehend. A simple power failure and my expensive toys serve me no more.

In the darkness on the bridge of the *North Sea* that first night in 1938, the instruments I now take for granted were decades beyond the horizon of common knowledge. Radios were there, but they were large vacuum tube affairs, filled with the static of uncertainty and failure. While we slept, the ship and every soul aboard swung up the Strait of Georgia guided only by the watchful eyes, ears, and experience of men who knew their trade. They watched a compass dimly lit by a small red bulb that told them the direction in which they were bound. In a time when personal competence was "Master of the Ship," the compass was all they had, save for the charts provided them and a thin manila line with a lead weight on the end. It could be thrown out to check the depth of unknown shallows should they stray from the beaten track.

In those years, dead reckoning was the sovereign of navigators. It was a seemingly simple and logical method of crossing the pathless oceans of the world. Both art and science, dead reckoning navigation depended on the measurement of such factors as time, distance, direction and speed. The results were "hard line" figures, calculations of the human mind thus not prone to electrical failure. There was a twist, however. The "art" portion of the process involved measuring the immeasurable, a sensing of tides, currents, winds, waves, and a sixth sense for the proximity of danger. With these mysterious variables, dead reckoning held much of the occult and thus became the province of those very few born to virtually "sense" the sea. Among these gifted individuals was Anthony Nickerson, Master of the *North Sea*.

As I remember him, Nickerson was a heavy-set, smallish man with beetle brows. He was self-assured beyond his size and a close friend of my stepfather to be. He was also a practical joker of coast-wide renown in a time when practical jokes were legendary. Oscar Larson had obtained our tickets in secret, fearing some kind of trickery from Nickerson and his crew. There were rumors of the marriage, but our identity was masked by the fact that I accompanied my mother on the trip. No one knew that Larson had contracted not only for a bride, but for a ready-made child as well. Had she been alone, she would have been instantly targeted as the bride to be. Over half a century ago, very few young women headed for Alaska in late August.

If Nickerson were the joker he was purported to be, the joking stopped on the bridge. At the invitation of some members of the crew, I was invited to spend some precious hours there sequestered in a far corner. I had also been advised by my mother to keep my mouth shut and learn. On several occasions, I was the subject of the skipper's unsolicited glance but he never spoke to me nor openly recognized the fact that I was there. The roaming giant ignored me and, being thoroughly intimidated, I was deeply grateful for the smallest and farthest corner in the wheel house, a beautiful sanctuary of polished mahogany and brass. Language there was always clean and concise, an economy of words cut from a prevailing silence. The Captain barked out curt orders that bounced like gunshots across the quiet of the bridge. The quartermaster responded by maintaining a course of incredible fineness, making corrections with a spoke or two of the wheel. There was something vaguely reminiscent of a penguin about Nickerson, probably his white shirt and dark blue uniform coat. He strode back and forth, crossing the margins of the wheel house with an intensity that made even the compass tilt his way. I noticed his officers took great care not to impede his path. Nor was he a stranger to the bridge wing in foul weather. Ignoring the warmth and comfort of the wheelhouse, I saw him often on the far reaches of the open bridge facing the driving rain with his head drawn downward into his body. Sometimes discomfort was necessary if one were to read the tides, currents, winds and drift, the imponderables of the art of dead reckoning navigation.

The Inland Passage to Alaska is a path of magnificence with vistas wide enough to draw the breath and close enough to touch. It is bounded on the East by mountains and forests of singular size and on the West by a complexity of islands defying poetic description. Some are immense and some seem too small to stand alone. They rise here and there from an inland sea filled with the richness of evergreen forests and the blues of dark coves. This is a place of eagles and owls and the place for a spirit to rest. Danger lurks here as well. Shallows, rocks, reefs, and false passages search for moments of distraction or inattention. It is well to reckon the cost of passages through this beauty in coins of constant vigilance. There is no margin for error. In fine weather it is a place where one tiptoes with a canoe or a cruise ship. At night or in fog, a misstep or error will surely threaten destruction.

Points North

Only a few hundred feet away up the wooden walkway called Creek Street, the little whorehouses of Ketchikan huddled in the rain.

My hours and days were now so filled with discovery there was seldom time for anything else. We threaded our way north through calm seas trespassing through Discovery Passage and Johnstone Strait where Killer Whales and Osprey were not a rarity but an hourly offering. The journey was well planned to meet the needs of a smooth-water sailor. The ship glided through a sheltered water world between a constantly fascinating corridor of rocky beaches and low granite banks. Huge stands of cedar, fir and spruce carpeted the passing land masses. The tops of the highest mountains were crowned with snow which filled their heavy crags and dusted the trees at timberline with rime lace. I never tired of watching the changing shores, staring breathlessly from time to time with the certainty that I saw some movement here or there marking the hiding place of a cougar or a bear. We passed small white lighthouses that told of their loneliness in the voices of foghorns or deep clanging bells. Miles and miles apart in small clearings on the shore stood humble homesteads. They marked the half-filled dreams of those who had come there, those who had labored, those who would stay awhile, and those who would then go away. Occasionally the wistful waving of a shore-bound child marked our passage, fading quickly into invisibility in the mist of half-rain that enveloped us. It was a daily drama of endless beauty, interest, and pathos until nightfall brought down the curtain.

I saw myself as a budding mariner and longed for some rough weather. I got my wish as the ship began a brief transit of Queen Charlotte Sound. I recall looking toward the West and seeing the "real ocean" as the last sheltering land mass fell astern. The sea now assumed that gray, wolfish color it adopts when it has room to roam. A northwesterly wind set the gulls to laboring and tore the tops off the waves which began to crash and splinter against our port side. It was weather in which one put up his collar and wore a hat. My sanctuary on the stern assumed the motion of a busy store elevator and became at once more animated and less dry. For some time we pitched into a moderate swell from the Northwest and, though some took to their bunks, I proudly weathered what was really a very moderate passage. The adolescent master mariner, who already considered himself a blue water sailor, would get sick soon enough.

Our course took advantage of every bit of shelter available, but there was another stretch of open ocean which had to be faced. Dixon Entrance begins abeam of Prince Rupert, British Columbia, and extends perhaps 50 miles north to the southern end of Prince of Wales Island. This was the longest and roughest stretch of open water we would encounter on the trip. Huge waves roll in off the North Pacific and rush southwest past the land mass of Cape Muzon. From Clarence Strait and Cordova Bay, massive tidal currents run southward to meet the ocean swell. Together these forces form a welter of disturbed sea that constitutes an object of respect for the master mariner and a problem area for the sunshine sailor. On May 14, 1936, the *North Sea* had struck a reef here in early morning fog. Damage was minor but, had the weather been rough, the accident could have been a major disaster. Both my mother and I fell victims to seasickness here as did many others.

The crossing of this stretch of water was a bit of maritime reality therapy in which the patient discovers he's not on the couch to be analyzed, he's on the couch because he's too sick to stand up. Years of living have convinced me that if one can avoid mal-de-mer, he or she is infinitely the richer for that avoidance. One can usually depend on Dixon Entrance to add the salt and pepper necessary to spice up the serenity of the Inland Passage. It didn't let us down. In years ahead this place would grant me an incomparable personal adventure, but for now all aboard took solace from the fact that the crossing was finished. Now sheltered by the mass of Prince of Wales Island, there would be a few hours of relative calm before the vessel blew its whistle announcing imminent arrival at the city of Ketchikan. Fortunately, it was a period of time just long enough to get things cleaned up.

Creek Street - Ketchikan

My recollections of Ketchikan are of wooden sidewalks, roughly dressed men and women, and lots of bars and curio stores with false fronts. It was a little like Dodge City, Kansas, only soaking wet. The shops specialized in selling totem poles, moccasins and mukluks made by native people who didn't get paid enough then and don't get paid enough now. With Captain Nickerson on the bridge wing giving orders, the *North Sea* gently settled next to a pier in the center of town. Tugs were a luxury and not needed. Docking in close confines was an art form with which the Alaskan steam ship skipper had better be acquainted. Complicated by a vicious little run of tide, this landing was a piece of master craftsmanship.

We looked down from the deck on a rather large crowd of rugged individuals who looked back up at us and waited purposefully for someone to wave at or for something to arrive. There was a difference about people here, a domination of simplicity without ornamentation dictated by the land in which they found themselves. A pervasive feeling of competence, confidence and independence filled the place and seemed mirrored in the faces of the people who lived here. Men, women, and children dressed to live with the weather and equipped themselves to beat adversity. It was to be expected. In the midst of a depression, an economic disaster that had been long lasting and devastating, these people had survived. They had survived in an environment of harsh weather, isolation, and a deprivation far more intense than that to be found "outside." Ketchikan was no town for a dabbler in life. It was essential for those who lived there to bond with the land and its weather. This bonding was more than a life style, it was a down payment on survival.

There was nothing dressed-up about the place. It was utilitarian, functional, and made out of bare boards. In Ketchikan and all other Alaskan towns a forest of fishing boat masts complemented the landscape. They lay bunched in close-by coves; their aggregate looking like a giant sleeping porcupine. Not a very pretty sight. There was the smell of fish that hadn't been sold in time and the sight of boats that hadn't been painted in time, then finally hadn't been painted at all. But they could float, and they could fish, and that was surely enough for that time and place.

A few light airplanes tied to a log float added romance to every Alaskan town. Most had become too old and too raunchy to fly in the states. They came up from Seattle coughing, wheezing and jumping like frogs from one backwoods landing strip to another. The men who flew them could also fix them and keep them going. The airplanes were tough and utilitarian like the people and the towns they served. Old and unwashed Curtiss Robins, Stinson Reliants and Lockeed Vegas squatted on pontoons in the murky water and dripped oil from cylinder head gaskets that had flown too long and would fly even longer. Like the boats, they were working machines. The utility of the ax, the rifle and the airplane were essential here. Aside from costly emergency flights, steamers like the *North Sea* were the only other link to the outer world. People used planes like taxicabs or busses; they needed ships to survive.

———

Upon arrival, the crew removed the hatch covers on the forward well deck as quickly as possible. The ship began the process of unloading or loading or both. The purser went through the ship banging on a three-toned gong and advised the passengers of the approximate length of the stay. By dint of common sense, they were expected to be on board when the mooring lines were let go. To lessen the possibility of stranding paying passengers, the steam whistle blew a half hour before an intended departure. It didn't always help. In spite of the warning, there were trinkets to be bought, there were sights to see and there were drinks to be finished. Departures were exciting. On occasions I watched individuals and groups running breathlessly toward the pier as the distance between the ship and the dock increased first by inches, then by feet. It's fun to think that at least once someone got wet. It is a certainty that more than once people were left behind.

My mother and I strolled through the town only briefly. We were held on a tether of fear that we might be left behind in a strange and unfamiliar albeit fascinating place. A walk of a couple of blocks took us to a small bridge where we witnessed the beginning of the spawning run of salmon heading up Ketchikan Creek. The water boiled with life from so many fish that the top layer could not get in the water. It was my first sight of a phenomenon that would become commonplace but always wondrous in the years ahead. Only a few hundred feet away up the wooden walkway called Creek Street, the little whorehouses of Ketchikan huddled in the rain. My questions about the buildings and their clientele prompted a sooner than anticipated return to the security of the *North Sea*.

Within an hour or two of our return there was the sound of hatch covers slamming down and the warning whistle blew calling the exploring tourists back to their floating nest. This time all made it back in time clutching totem poles, moccasins or mukluks and bragging about the prices they'd paid. Some bore an additional load of refreshments that had changed their gait from a souvenir stroll to a dampened stagger. Their handicap increased noticeably as they climbed the gangplank which had risen steeply to near vertical by a rising tide.

We departed Ketchikan and continued to elbow our way north through Clarence Strait. The passing panorama of towering mountains, evergreens, and small coves, bays and islands was a constantly changing and endlessly fascinating experience. There was often a pelting rain coming straight down in a dense and relentless torrent. Rain storms in Alaska seemed to be more intense than anywhere else. The water fell as if poured from a bucket, then seemed to bounce back up from the earth to cloak the underbrush and branches of firs in a ghostly mist. On this afternoon I saw my first bear. It was a small black one, a cub perhaps. Head down and browsing, his pigeon-toed walk carried him along the beach for perhaps twenty yards. He swung a too-small head toward the gliding ship and stared briefly at us from a distance of perhaps two hundred yards. The sight fascinated me and I wanted to freeze-frame the moment. Then, without panic and in seeming disinterest, he turned and ambled back into the underbrush beside a great granite boulder. My eyes riveted at the spot hoping for another sighting, but the ship moved inexorably up the passage and in a minute or two the boulder and the bear disappeared forever in the mist. I told my mother and others of the sighting, but they seemed singularly unimpressed. I had done a lot of shoreline staring; the sighting was important to me.

Heading east at the south end of Zarembo Island, we rounded a rocky point and swung northeast again, up Stikene Strait. We turned right and, in an hour docked gently at the fishing village of Wrangell at the mouth of the Stikene River. The Stikene forms a water pathway leading east to the fog-shrouded interior highlands of British Columbia. A

primitive culture flourished in the mists of these islands eons ago. For millennia, an ancient people hunted, fished, and gathered in the shelter and peace of the surrounding bays and inlets. In a prehistoric era they had crossed the land bridge between Siberia and Alaska and used the Stikene River as a regular transportation artery long before the founding of the early civilizations of Egypt and Sumeria.

In a yellowed letter written to my mother over a quarter century ago, my mother and stepfather's close friend Clyda Schott Greely wrote of her father and the Wrangell area: *"My father Louis Schott was a pioneer cannery man in Alaska. He went to Wrangell in 1887 with Bob Bell to build a cannery for R. D. Hume at the mouth of the Stikene River. My first trip to Alaska was in 1899. Spent the summer at Kodiak Island-the westward. We traveled in sailing ships...a fascinating life."* Clyda and her family knew Alaska as a truly wild and pristine land waiting, as did all the West, to yield riches to those strong enough to claim them. In early days, these tiny towns like Wrangell existed as mere enclaves, small clearings in a wilderness. They were isolated by seemingly endless stands of immense fir, spruce and cedar trees and a head-high barricade of nearly impenetrable and perpetually dripping undergrowth. It's truly difficult to imagine the primitive quality of the lives led and the hardships endured by these entrepreneur-adventurer-beginners.

Winters were bitterly cold and summers brought little sunshine. In this place which births storms, lasting mists, winds, and falling rain are a constant. Tents were a lifestyle and the food fare was hard to obtain, simple and wild. A few days of warmth and sunshine brought forth black clouds of stinging and biting insects which clogged the eyes, ears and nose of their victims. The infestation reduced men and animals to near madness.

These searchers for a future hand-carved the beginnings of a fishing industry that has transfigured the Alaskan Coastline and the Pacific Northwest for a hundred years.

From Wrangell, the path northward led through the slim confines of Wrangell Narrows, one of the narrowest passages on the journey. Graveled shores were so close aboard, it was as if we walked the beaches on either side of the now slowly creeping steamer. The details of rocks and small shorebirds became incredibly visible in the closeness. Feeding gulls fluttered nervously, hovering as we passed and returned to their normal world of hunt and peck only after they had vanished in the mists astern. At the head of the Narrows lay the small town of Petersburg. This town was different. It was started by, and named in honor of Peter Thams Buschmann. In a few days my mother's impending marriage would put me in close contact with the sons and grandsons of its founder. Though it seems a digression, the story of the beginnings of my association with the Buschmann family must begin here.

The history of the Buschmann family is linked inextricably to the history of Alaska and its fishing industry. Both are stories of triumph and tragedy, wealth, and ruin. There is a novel in the lives of this family, many of whom lived lives so poignant and so fraught with good and ill fortune that it seems a fiction. If I am to tell a story of boats and Alaska, the Buschmann family is the rock upon which the story must rest. The thread of them runs through the time of my story, and the two are so intertwined that separation is totally impossible. I face a dichotomy here. I loved a few of these people. Time has mitigated my disappointment in some of the others.

Peter Thams Buschmann, his wife Petra, and their children immigrated to the United States from Aure, Norway, in 1891. He was forty-one years of age when he arrived in Tacoma, Washington, seeking a new life and a new beginning. Of the couple's children, five were boys: Christian Henrik was the oldest, then came August, followed by Eigel, Trygve and Leif Christie. Four girls appear on a family tree as offspring of Peter and Petra. In order of birth they were Elisabeth, Solveig, Sophie, and Ruth.

In Norway, Peter the scion of the clan, had been a successful fisherman and fish processor. He built several herring saltery plants along the Norwegian coast and dealt in the wholesale marketing of Atlantic Salmon. He was an extremely hard driven, inventive and energetic man, who was tailor-made for the rough and tumble business he had chosen to pursue in Norway and later in his adopted land. In Alaska he began to build an empire with four of his sons, Christian, August, Eigel and Leif. Trygve worked in the business in the early years but was more academically oriented. After graduation from the University of Pennsylvania, he pursued a successful career as a physician and surgeon in Seattle.

The family's business interests in Alaska prospered from the beginning. The infant empire began to expand with great promise. Fishing traps were built and produced sudden wealth. Petersburg, their town, grew and prospered. The father and brothers acquired fish trap locations which would produce incomes in the millions. Year after year produced more promise for the future and solid growth in the family's assets. After eleven years, and apparently feeling the time was right to withdraw from the burgeoning industry, Peter Buschmann sold out all the family's interest in the spring of 1902. All profits from the sale of the Buschmann properties were invested in stocks and bonds issued by the Pacific Packing and Navigation Company, a large combine of Northwest interests which promised even greater returns for their investments. The sale was the precursor of disaster.

At the time of the transaction, the Alaska Packers Association, a large and powerful company, maintained a virtual monopoly over the canned salmon trade. Seeing the upstart Pacific Packing and Navigation Company as a threat, they took the appropriate cut-throat action so typical of early American industry. In the fall of 1902, sensing a weak spot in the new company, Alaska Packers Association drastically dropped the price on pink salmon and flooded the market. The results were immediate. The Pacific Packing and Navigation Company, which had shown such initial promise, went bankrupt. For the Buschmann interests, it was devastating and the family found itself in financial ruin. All the opportunities which had presented themselves and all the labors that the family had put forth had profited them nothing. Their stock was worthless and their bond holdings were auctioned for five cents on the dollar. In 1903, apparently prompted by the toppling of his business interests, Peter Buschmann committed suicide.

Following a sheriff's sale of the assets of the now defunct PPNC, a new company was formed and named Northwestern Fisheries Company. Christian Henrik, Peter's oldest son assumed the role of general manager of the new company, and a secure and promising future seemed in the offing. In a tragic irony twelve years later, history repeated itself. Facing business losses, Christian Henrik Buschmann closed an office door in the Smith Tower of downtown Seattle, removed a revolver from his coat pocket, and killed himself.

Leif Christie, the youngest of Peter's sons, continued on in the salmon and herring business, serving in various managerial and entrepreneurial roles. In 1929, Leif purchased the cannery at Skowl Arm on Prince of Wales Island. He operated the cannery until he suffered a fatal heart attack in 1939, leaving a wife and two children. I met him but once or twice and scarcely knew him. Later, I would be close to his wife Esther, and their two children, Lorraine and Leif, both near my age. Thus, of the six Buschmann males, father and sons who had labored so hard and accomplished so much, only August, Eigel and Trygve remained.

The Buschmann girls were also star crossed by fate. Of the four, Solveig, Sophie, Elisabeth, and Ruth, I knew only Ruth, the youngest, born in 1890. I found her to be a pleasant, unobtrusive person whom I saw at Christmas time and at other family parties. At the time of my mother's marriage to Oscar,

Ruth was a staunch spinster of fifty. Separated by generations of time and social difference, I saw her as a nice old lady with whom I had little in common. I never met Elisabeth Buschmann, only the diminutive husband she left behind. Charles Beaumont Wykhan Piercy, her husband, was of lesser British peerage. He spoke with a gentle voice and was a delightfully polite individual who was always present at family gatherings. He was the last person in the world one might see as an adventurer but, appearances often deceive. Shortly after the turn of the century, he joined a British research party investigating primitive tribes in the headwaters of the Amazon River. At that time, this area was totally unexplored and fraught with danger. In the course of the expedition and in the heart of the remote Matto Grosso area of Brazil, the group was attacked by hostile natives. All of the expedition's supplies and weapons were lost, including the canoes which offered the only apparent avenue of escape. Two months later, after an epic land trek out of the jungle, two survivors out of thirty men who began the expedition stumbled into a remote village. Charles Beaumont Wykhan Piercy was one of them. The rest were never seen or heard of again.

I know nothing of the marriage of "Beau" and Elisabeth because it was never a topic of conversation. It was as if Beaumont existed as an individual, never in unison with a wife who was now gone. In retrospect, I sense now an almost tangible compulsion on the part of the family to avoid the presence of her memory. Oscar explained it to me later, shaking his head at the remembrance. In an enigmatic turn of events dreadful beyond belief, Elisabeth locked herself in a room and beyond help or assistance, destroyed herself. It was a death so tragic and bizarre that careful whispers on rare occasions gave only a hint of its horror. Understandably, it could only be treated as a thing that never happened by those who remained.

The following account of the early activities of the Buschmann family in Alaska is from a biographical sketch written by August Buschmann in January 1963. This chronicle paints a picture of men who were driven to succeed. In a primitive land and in a primitive time their strength and ingenuity brought them fortunes. The fates were not so kind to them. I quote:

Early in 1892, the family moved to Port Townsend where Father established a small saltery and smokehouse for herring and halibut. During that summer, Father and I also fished for halibut and codfish in the Straits off Port Townsend and delivered the fish by rowboat to a small retail fish market in Everett (about 30 miles distant), operated by my oldest brother, Christian Henrik. Everett was then in its infancy; it had mud streets and a few plank sidewalks at that time. In the late fall that year, we moved to Fairhaven (now part of Bellingham, Washington) where Father continued salting and smoking herring and halibut for the local market.

During the summer of 1894, he also built the first salmon fish trap on the West Coast of Lummi Island, close to Bellingham. This was accomplished by building a raft from logs to substitute for a pile-driver scow. We made the gins from hewn piling and used an iron ringed small log four feet long as a hammer, which we hoisted with a hand windlass. This venture was not very successful, since having very primitive equipment, we could not drive out far enough into the current and deep water to catch the heavy run of sockeye salmon. Years later, when modern equipment was used by others to drive into deeper water, this location became one of the best and caught millions of sockeye salmon.

In the early spring of 1895, Father and I went to Ketchikan, Alaska, on the steamer ALKI. Here father arranged for the use of a 60-foot sailing schooner called VOLUNTEER from which we with another man, fished and salted halibut in that area during the spring and early summer. In the early fall, we also located a cannery site at the entrance of Mink Arm, a branch of Boca De Quadra Inlet about forty miles southeast of Ketchikan, where Father built and operated his first salmon cannery in 1896. Later in the season of 1895, father and I fished dogfish and sharks for the livers, close to Loring Cannery north of Ketchikan. We extracted about sixty barrels of lubricating oil from these livers which we sold on the Seattle market.

In 1897 he also built and operated a mild-cure salting station for King salmon on Taku Inlet across from Taku Glacier. Early in 1898, Father located the Trade and Manufacturing site on which most of Petersburg is now located. Late in the spring of that year, on a trip from Boca DeQuadra Cannery, en route to the mild-curing saltery on Taku Inlet, he put me and an Indian named Paul ashore at this location with tools and enough lumber and shingles to build the location cabin on this Trade and Manufacturing site (now known as Petersburg), which was then legally necessary for validation. That summer and fall he commenced building the original dock, cannery, store, and living quarters. Later he built bunkhouses, shipways, a sawmill, and other facilities on this site, and put up the first pack of salmon there in 1900.

This location at the northern end of Wrangell Narrows was not selected exclusively as a salmon cannery location, but also as a location for a fresh halibut business, because glacier ice was conveniently available, which made the ideal location from which halibut could be iced, boxed, and shipped to the Seattle market. It was, and still is, on the direct inside steamer route to Seattle, and the ice from LaConte Glacier and Thomas Bay drifting into Wrangell Narrows in front of this site on almost every incoming tide provided the halibut fishermen with the ice so necessary for preserving their fresh fish for shipment to Seattle. Please remember that in the late 1890s and the early part of this century, there were no powered halibut schooners here, and they all (dozens of them), manned mostly by Norwegians, sailed the inside passage about 700 miles to Petersburg, from Puget Sound in the fall and back in the spring. Frederick Sound, bordering Wrangell Narrows to the north, was then one of the best, if not the best, large inside areas in Alaska for fishing halibut, and having the ice at their door made this location ideal for the halibut fishermen.

In 1897, Father also bought a salmon saltery location in Bartlett Cove, located at the entrance of Glacier Bay, Southeastern Alaska, not far from Muir Glacier at that time. In 1899 I operated the saltery there and caught the salmon, employing Hoonah natives. We packed about 680 barrels of Red salmon there that year. In the spring of 1901, Father sent me up to build and operate a salmon cannery in Sitkoh Bay at the entrance of Peril Straits, southeastern Alaska. The government required salmon hatcheries on the lakes above Basket Bay and Pavlof Harbor close by. He built a large cannery there and packed about 60,000 cases of salmon that year. During the winter of 1901 and spring of 1902, father and his associates sold all their Alaska interests, then held by the following companies: Quadra Packing Company, Petersburg Packing Company and Chatham Straits Packing Company, to a newly organized large cannery known as the Pacific Packing and Navigation Company which, on account of financial difficulties, went bankrupt in 1903."

In 1910, my stepfather Oscar's sister Mathelde, called "Teddy," married August Buschmann. Following the deaths of Peter and Christian Henrik, August assumed the "alpha role" in the family. He was a portly, intense man with thin wavy gray hair. He seldom separated himself from an expensive cigar. From the beginning, August and I seemed to have little in common. That relationship did not change over the years. Teddy, his wife, impressed me as a woman less than warm and perhaps less than totally pleased that my mother and I had joined even the outer circle of their extended family. As the years passed, it became increasingly clear that several members of the group shared that feeling.

I found Trygve Buschmann to be a difficult man to enjoy or admire. In my opinion, he was an imperious, tyrannical individual who extended kindness only toward those he recognized as being worthy of his attention. The circle of those chosen few was very small. If this appraisal seems hard, it also seems totally valid after half a century of introspection. Trygve and Katherine had two lovely and talented children. Bronson was exactly my age and Helen was two years younger. As the son and daughter of a successful and prominent Seattle physician, they traveled in social circles far different from mine. On every possible occasion, their father took pains to make that fact abundantly clear. When speech between us was unavoidable, he always addressed me with body language that indicated he was only passing time. With head drawn back, tilted and peering down his nose, he seemed to take delight in comparing me to his son and, in so doing to find me particularly wanting. The practice may have been justified, but was so brazen and transparent that it was evident to me as a child of fourteen. I wondered then why he did it. After fifty five more years of living, I still do.

Bronson was a talented violinist, and Helen was equally talented on the piano. Both were sufficiently gifted to aspire to concert careers. As children we associated on the adult fringe of family parties. I recall them both as being "nice kids," pleasant to be around. They lived in a large and pretentious home in a fine neighborhood, and Bronson had a twenty-foot Chris Craft runabout aptly named the *Bronson B*. I saw the speedboat once or twice, but due to circumstances, never got a ride in it. At fourteen I recall wondering how it was for them to live with a father who seemed a total despot. I held empathic feelings for both of them and realized how truly fortunate I was, even if I didn't have a speedboat.

If there were a coldness and non-caring aspect to some members of the Buschmann family it stopped with August's younger brother, Eigel. From our first meeting, he extended a friendship to me that I have valued all my life. He and his spouse, Nora had five children, four boys and one girl. Of the four boys I would become very close to two of them, Richard and Norman. The other two boys, Frederick and Robert, were older than I and traveled in different circles. I expect Eigel's tolerance and acceptance of me was partially initiated by the fact that he liked kids that liked boats. He also had a warmth and compassion which prompted him to bend over and make eye contact when he talked with young people who were shorter than he was. That's important for any tall person to do.

Eigel Buschmann was a long and lean man. Handsome in his early years, the creases he developed with age were all in the right places, and granted him the dignity he deserved. His posture was exceedingly erect, he stood about six foot two or three, and looked taller. Essentially a tough fisherman, circumstances beyond his control had polished him to a managerial shine and kicked him upstairs so to speak. A rough and tough seine boat skipper in his early days, there were rumors that he was not above removing fish from someone else's traps if the night were dark and conditions just right. As General Superintendent of Nakat Packing Corporation, he now spent his time in an office and board room. From our talks and the times we spent together, I'm sure he preferred the old days and the flying bridge of a cannery tender or seine boat chasing salmon. My step-father described him as a skipper of consummate skill. A love of boats was something Eigel and I shared for as long as he lived.

In retrospect, I orbited most of the Buschmann family from light years away. It wasn't necessarily through choice, just that there was never enough warmth to bring me in closer. At a hundred family gatherings, a long hesitation and mental search occurred before they pulled my name from the files of their collective minds. With some of them it took longer than others. I was a child seeking some degree of belonging and found their subtle rejection and non-caring attitude to be somewhat hurtful. It was a new experience for me since I had come from a home where love and acceptance had been a way of life. When I had matured a bit and entered high school, their studied forgetfulness and disinterest became something to be smiled at or ignored. I ceased trying to help them recall that I was around or that my name was Eddie.

But, on that first trip North, our stay in Petersburg was short, only a few hours as I recall. The ritual of departure did not vary. Hatch covers were secured, the steam whistle belted out its message, and passengers scurried aboard at the last minute. The *North Sea* backed away from the dock and swung northward through Frederick Sound and Stephans Passage. The next stop would be Juneau, Alaska, and the new life that Oscar Larson had promised to my mother and to me.

We arrived at Juneau early in the morning, and docked shortly after dawn. Needless to say we were up and dressed. Oscar waited on the dock in a light rain that did nothing to dampen his spirits or my mother's or mine. Captain Nickerson high on the bridge wing picked out Oscar's figure on the dock and waited until the gangplank was lowered to determine which of his passengers would be the future bride. He roared when he determined that it was the young woman with the scrawny kid. His first words after greeting Oscar were, "Hell, If I'd known it was the woman with the kid, I'd sure as hell have left them in Petersburg." I'm sure he spoke the truth.

Photograph of the cannery at Port Althorp when it operated as the Deep Sea Canning Company under the direction and ownership of August Buschmann.
In the early 1930's the cannery and docking was completely refurbished by the Alaska Pacific Salmon Company, a subsidiary of the Skinner and Eddy Corporation. The cannery burned to the ground in 1940 and was not rebuilt.

Port Althorp

I often pondered the liklihood that I was the first person to stop, stand and gaze at this or that particular place since the beginning of time.

My mother and Oscar were married on the morning of the seventh day of September 1938 by the United States Commissioner for the Territory of Alaska. The next day it rained, and about noon the *North Sea* slipped her dock lines, rounded the north end of Admiralty Island and headed up Icy Strait. Some seventy miles later, we turned south into Cross Sound. I saw the clustered buildings of Port Althorp from a long way off. They rose from an endless sea of spruce, fir and cedar, and huddled together on the north shore of the bay beneath mountains which seemed to scrape the sky. There was a new world of wonder here waiting to be explored, and the majesty and beauty of the spot is as much a part of me now as it was the first time I was privileged to see it in the light rain of an early September evening.

Our quarters were spacious and comfortable occupying the second floor of a building housing the cannery office and a small "company store" which provided necessities for people working at the cannery. We were sandwiched between two large and impressive warehouses which afforded some protection from a wind which blew with spectacular regularity. From the living room window the view across the bay was monumental. An endless chain of mountains stretched to the north and south with tops covered by snow that never melted. Although still early in September, the cold was becoming a noticeable thing. Just out of sight twenty miles to the North, five huge glaciers slid slowly seaward calving gigantic icebergs into Glacier Bay, which is now the site of a National Park of the same name. When the winds blew from that direction, it was weather for heavy jackets and a night time tucking of blankets. Rain was a staple of this land. It was accepted and expected, a way of life. It was logical that sunshine should appear only rarely in a place where the storms of the northern hemisphere are born.

The next morning after our arrival I was to discover that I was not the only kid in this remote place. Barbara Brandmier, daughter of the Cannery Foreman, was about four or five years old at the time. She lived with her mother and father in a small house a quarter mile away from ours. Our age difference immediately shut out any close association. In retrospect I sense how difficult it must have been for a little girl in such a place. She surely experienced a constant yearning for companionship and playmates. At that time I was completely disdainful of small children and needed no one like her to clutter up the greatest adventure of my life. Her most overt attempt to establish communication were the dandelion rings she left for me at the front door to our apartment. Needless to say they were totally ignored and after a bit she quit trying and returned to what must have been a crushing loneliness with only seagulls, her dolls, and not much else for company. Strangely, in a place so alien to the interests of a little girl, I never saw her cry.

August Buschmann built the cannery in 1917 and 1918 long before the dawn of plywood and other materials of building expediency. In those days, in that place, construction meant the joining of wood, nails, and glass in a strong and practical fashion. Function was paramount and there was no time for frills. All interior walls of our apartment were covered with tongue and groove ship-lap giving the appearance of a sea-going cabin. It had been built carefully to withstand the rigors of winters when temperatures fell to below zero, and heavy winds from

This photograph shows the main cannery buildings at Port Althorp. The Superintendent's quarters were located on the second floor of the center building with rounded roof.

the West blew across the sound. The unusually heavy joists, rafters and timbers were transported by barge from Juneau during construction. Since Juneau was close to a hundred miles away, the trip took many hours. Twenty springs and summers of hard usage and twenty winters of bitter winds and cold had not dampened or dented the place. It seemed invincible.

Inside, the lightly stained and shellacked walls were warm with color and texture; pure unpainted wood "belonged" to this building and to this primitive place. There was a large living room and an ample kitchen that was rarely used. We took all our meals in the "Blue Room" of the mess hall, a block away. It was a separate dining room used by the Superintendent, his family, and any visiting guests or dignitaries. The Blue Room was also an object of some derision by cannery personnel. It served to bolster the feeling of a "class" society. I felt this sensitivity almost at once and was a little uncomfortable about it. The following year, when I began working on the *Doris E,* I chose to have most of my meals in the regular mess hall and felt better about it.

In addition to the rooms already mentioned, our apartment had two large bedrooms, a bathroom and a small store room. The furniture was Spartan, most of it heavy traditional oak done in the style of the 1920's. Like the building, the furniture spoke of practicality and utility...no flowers or fluff. In the living room, on a small table close by Dad's chair,

Deer feed in spring among the cannery buildings. They were the only company for a lonely winter watchman.

was a Zenith Transoceanic Radio. It was designed to pick up short-wave and standard broadcasting frequencies which, aside from visitors and the steamer, constituted our only real tie to the outside. A large, free-standing wood stove provided more than adequate heat and made the entire apartment comfortably warm on the coldest and wettest of nights. It was a very pleasant place to live and I recognized it as "home" from the beginning.

There was some disappointment for me when we arrived. There were no cannery tenders to be seen. All the boats were involved in closing activities for the coming winter. Opening and closing a salmon cannery always involved a flurry of activity. Time was of the essence now with bad weather just around the corner. Anchors of the massive fish traps had to be raised and stored, and the traps towed to sheltered moorings at the head of the bay. There were dozens of other tasks which the tenders had to complete before heading south for the winter. In their absence, I had a couple of days to explore the cannery and close-in wilderness.

An enormous dock was the salient feature of the cannery. It extended far into the bay and supported many of the cannery buildings. Tides in Alaska are enormous. The only larger tides on earth occur in the Bay of Fundy off the coast of Eastern Canada. Cannery docks had to extend far enough from the shore to provide sufficient draft for steamer service, even at low tide. I recall the wharf area of the cannery to be the equivalent in square footage of perhaps two large city blocks requiring hundreds of support pilings. Everything about the area was massive and strongly built to support the warehouse and cannery buildings and the attendant activity.

During daylight hours, the dock area hummed with action. Fork lift trucks shuttled back and forth with pallets loaded with cases of salmon. Boat crews moved large nets to and from the pier on heavy iron wheeled carts. Groups of cannery workers, in white aprons, took smoke breaks and told dirty jokes as they relished a few minutes respite from the roar of canning machines. Deck hands, pushing hand trucks, wheeled barrels of lube oil or grease to waiting seine boats or trollers. There was always something going on. People seemed to scurry from one place to another, sensing the need to get the job done and get the hell south where they belonged before the snow began to fall. At Port Althorp time was reckoned by weather and tides as much as it was by the clock. If one had to work twenty-four hours straight to complete a job, it was the expected thing to do.

As one looked at the cannery from the bay, the most striking features were three huge, gabled, three-story buildings. They were dominant and screened all the lesser buildings from view. Two stories of the first building on the right were devoted to canning machines and incoming fish storage bins. The top or gabled portion contained a "web loft" where fish netting, seines, spiller web and cordage were stored. Next to the cannery building on the left, was a smaller two-story structure containing the store and office on the first floor and our apartment on the second.

To the left of this building stood two more huge warehouse buildings designed for labeling and packing purposes; they also contained thousands of cases of salmon, each case containing 48 one-pound tall cans, awaiting shipment south. The large warehouses were about seventy feet wide by two-hundred feet long, painted white with green trim. The fronts of these buildings appeared rather "barn like," since large double doors faced out from each floor through which nets and heavy equipment could be stored or removed.

Behind these primary buildings was a row of smaller structures that housed facilities essential to the cannery's operation. On the right stood a two-story building housing large boilers and the steam power plant that provided power for all the canning machinery. Steam also drove an electric generator used for lighting the entire cannery and dock area. It was a little noisy, but the sound soon blended into the life style and became quite unnoticeable. In 1938 in Alaska, industrial power transmission had changed little since the design of the steam engine and the beginning of the industrial revolution. The coal-fired steam plant produced power which was then delivered to machinery through a series of overhead belts and pulleys. Ceilings of rooms housing machinery were covered by a maze of these pulleys and shafts. Turning through primitive bearings, the pulleys drove the machines by use of wide leather belts.

Oscar Larson at Port Althorp Spring, 1927

When no canning was in process, the overhead pulleys and idling belts filled these rooms with a soft, energetic whirring sound. During the actual canning process, the noise was deafening. Each machine contributed a patterned rhythm of clanks, clunks, and clatter until the synergistic effect melted into a constant mechanical roar.

Some of the steam developed to drive machinery was also diverted to heat huge retorts. These retorts served as steam pressure cookers. Large galvanized trays filled with canned salmon were wheeled into the retorts and cooked for a period lasting shortly over an hour. Following this cooking, the cans were then put aside to cool and to be loaded into cases for shipment south. Port Althorp was equipped with six cylindrical retorts about six feet in diameter and twenty feet in length. At the height of the canning season, all machinery operated twenty-four hours per day and the retorts constantly disgorged racks which held thousands of steaming silver cans of salmon.

To the left of the power plant stood a machine shop and carpenter shop. Each was capable of repairing and/or replacing critical elements of the cannery operation. In the event of steam plant failure, some emergency power was provided by small, slow speed diesel engines, and portable generators. Interestingly, the elevators used to lift fish from the boats and barges to the cannery building were powered by water wheels, as were the large freight elevators in the warehouses. Water-wheel power was developed in the dawn of history, and these Pelton water wheels were highly refined examples of their age-old predecessors. They were thoroughly reliable and, when geared down, they produced tremendous torque and could accomplish many heavy jobs.

To the right and the left of the dock area and cannery complex were floats for boat moorage. Because of the severe tides, these floats were essential. At times it was necessary to moor a boat to a piling. If such was the case, the boat had to be tied with a "slip line." A slip line is a mooring line which is looped loosely around the piling, thus allowing the craft to rise or fall freely with the tide. Horror stories abounded relating instances when boats were improperly moored or tied to a piling too tightly. In a swing of tide, an unwary skipper might return after a couple of hours absence to discover his boat hanging from a dock face or, perhaps worse, completely submerged. Slip lines were a lesson learned early.

Caucasian and Oriental or Filipino workers were served and housed in a segregated mess hall and a two story bunk house located on the shore behind the dock area. The radio shack, located a hundred yards to the right, was connected to the dock area by a wooden walk way. It was a two story structure containing the radio room and quarters for its operator, referred to always as "Sparks." Our radio still spoke primarily in the language of the telegraph key, but voice transmission was possible with some of the cannery tenders if the boats weren't too far away.

Radio transmitters and receivers of the day were huge black boxes filled with vacuum tubes. They were invariably dusty and always smelled as if the wires were burning. At Port Althorp, the pre-war radio equipment took most of the wall space in a rather large room. Some years we had highly skilled radio operators, but in 1938 we were stuck with one so inept we could have done better with a tin can and a waxed string. Working one night on a receiver, he sealed his own fate. Finding the task particularly exasperating he verbally vented his wrath through a transmitter he didn't know was open. Unfortunately, the receiver in our living room was tuned to the same frequency and the room was suddenly filled with words that we didn't use around my mother. Dad fired him the next day and hired a more capable replacement from Ketchikan for the remainder of the season.

Behind the bunkhouses, situated on a small rise, were ten or fifteen small cabins which served as quarters for Native American seine boat crews. These cabins were barely adequate for one or two people but of-

A Chichagof "Brownie," hungry from winter denning, seeks quarters of beef aging under the powerhouse eaves.

ten housed many more. The resident population was always changing, and ranged in age from the ancient to the new born. Native Americans, mostly of Tlinget background, excelled as fishing boat skippers and crew members. They were an aloof people and operated their own boats in their own manner. Unless spoken to, they never spoke. I don't recall a single dialogue I ever had with a Tlinget at Port Althorp; it was my fault more than theirs. I am not proud of that.

Behind the "native quarters," as they were referred to, a small wooden walkway crossed Margaret Creek, and paralleled a flume that led into the woods. The flume itself was of wood and banded-iron construction, about a foot and a half in diameter and punctuated at intervals with small leaks surrounded by attendant green moss. The flume and walkway gently rose from the rear of the cannery and crossed verdant brush, bogs and meadows until both terminated perhaps a mile from the cannery at a small dam. The dam and flume constituted the cannery's entire fresh water supply. Much of the walkway was raised off the spongy ground, in some places as much as ten feet, while other sections ran for several hundred yards at ground level. In my periodic inspections of the "pipeline," the ground level segments of the pipe triggered me with a special degree of alertness.

The flume which provided water for the cannery is here seen running from near the dam to the cannery which is over the hill in the background. The flume ran through prime bear country and was always an exciting journey.

I had been warned of the danger of bears. The one I had seen from the *North Sea* on the beach near Wrangell had been relatively small and black. The bears of Chichagof Island were Brown Bears that were huge, unpredictable and life-threatening. I never went up the pipeline without one of my most prized possessions, a single shot Remington .22 rifle. I knew, of course, that such a weapon constituted no threat whatever to an angry Alaskan Brown Bear, but it just felt good to have it along. In my childhood imagination I was subject to some weird fantasies. On several occasions I recall picturing myself standing alone in a sunlit meadow and facing the lethal charge of a two-ton "Brownie." I would wait until the last second, raise the .22 to my scrawny shoulder, and with unerring accuracy shoot the charging carnivore through the left eye. The bullet would enter the creature's brain, and he would fall dead at my feet. I really didn't think that would ever happen, but in those days I spent a lot of time creating images which pleased me.

Some bear stories lacked any semblance of humor. A few weeks before we arrived at the cannery a tragic event had occurred. A young homesteader and his wife had built a cabin close to the beach about five miles north of the cannery site. The couple had a small daughter perhaps three or four years old. They worked hard to make the place go. He had done some hand trolling for salmon selling his few fish to the cannery for badly needed cash. The family was well liked and shopped at the cannery store for necessities from time to time. One evening in late August, just before dark, the husband went out for evening firewood. The pile of cut and split firewood was about fifty yards from the cabin door. A browsing female Brown bear with a small cub wandered between him and the cabin. According to his wife, he shouted and attempted to scare the bear off, then started to run toward the cabin for a rifle. The bear dragged him down and killed him in full view of his wife and child. The trauma was so great the woman and her little girl abandoned the cabin. Dreams of the homestead and the future died less than fifty yards from their front door. They departed shortly afterward, and presumably left the island forever.

In the days ahead, I was always careful in my tentative explorations of the wildness just beyond the cannery site. I much preferred the raised portions of the walkway which put one at least a little out of harm's way. But, it was the ground level stretches that offered the adventure and the adrenaline rush

The *dam at Port Althorp lay at the east end of the flume about a mile from the cannery. It was a beautiful site and the author visited it many times carrying his .22 caliber rifle to ward off any huge bears that might impede his way. I still recall the peace and quiet of this magic place and the solitude I found there.*

of a possible bear confrontation. Savoring the excitement and the sense of danger, I was watchful when crossing these areas, and ready to break into a dead run. The pipeline walk was a favorite. One moment there would be the overwhelming sound of canning machinery, voices, and the barking of a native dog; after fifty yards of pipe line walking, one passed into another world and entered the silence and beauty of a primeval, unexplored forest so boundless it defied imagination. I was thrilled at the prospect.

I experienced acute awareness on some of my walks. I could stare far into the hills beyond the dam and the narrow pipeline and know that it was virgin country. No one had ever walked that way before. Beyond me there was a wealth of unknown land, a thousand valleys, meadows and trout streams to explore, just for the walking! I was too young and too afraid for real exploration; it was like being afraid of the dark. On occasion though, I would venture some little way from the beaten track and pause beside a creek or meadow. I often pondered the likelihood that I was the first person to stop, stand and gaze at this or that particular place since the beginning of time. It was a new, wondrous and unforgettable experience, and another memory to treasure.

The Doris E

There was the rush of compressed air—then the first ignition—the birth of firing—the clatter of push rods and valves, and then the smell and sound of raw, sweet, power.

The *Doris E* was built in Port Blakely Washington in 1927. She was 85 feet in length and powered by a Washington Estep diesel engine of 185 horsepower. If there was ever a craft to be loved, it was this handsome towboat which has provided a lifetime of memories for the author.

Several days of exploring had already convinced me that Port Althorp was a very special place, but the best was yet to come. Earlier in this story I drew attention to life interests that are peculiar to one individual or another. It seems to me that the penchant to identify with certain objects or situations may well lie in the genes. I hold that this capacity

Fred Foster, cook on the *Doris E*, prepares king crab on the afterdeck. At the time of this photograph, Fred was 84 years of age, and cooked every day for the crew of the boat. He was a poet and philosopher, deeply admired by the author.

for identification is as inborn and irrefutable as fallen arches or cavities. It is inescapable. Such identification with an inanimate object or objects demands that the individual involved be something of a dreamer, and that he or she automatically grants "life" to those special targets of his or her affection. All my life I have had a compelling interest in boats. I have always seen them as transcending the wood, glass, and steel of which they are made. The joy in my life is seeing them as living entities possessing varying personalities, quirks, and habits, some good—some bad. That may be a little bit crazy, but I'm stuck with it. I am convinced that boats are sea-beings, living out lives and creating fascinating histories from the adventures of their days. Since they live, inevitably like us, they also die. That is what I chose to believe as a child; that is what I prefer to believe now that I am older. I'm really secure in this thinking and too much a romantic to want that illusion destroyed.

What's more, there is a marvelous symbiosis which exists between boats and the men who sail and work them. The personalities of a craft and its crew are as interwoven as are their fates. In a place of bad weather and vicious seas, the interdependence of the two becomes very clear, and very real. I have seen it demonstrated on many occasions. The strength of the hull and the invincibility of the crew are indivisible entities; together they become more than the sum of their parts and, in the end, spell success or spell disaster.

Early in the morning I looked out the front window and saw, at last, the tall brown mast and boom of a cannery tender protruding above the edge of the wharf. I downed a bowl of cornflakes and ran down to the dock, putting on a jacket as I went. I peered over the 12 x 12 timber at the edge and looked down on the *Doris E*, riding a low tide and rising and falling gently on a slight morning swell. She looked immense and she was; broad beamed and 85 feet long, every inch a tow boat. A trickle of coffee-smelling smoke issued from the "Charlie Noble," the stack above her galley, but there wasn't a soul in sight. I climbed fifteen feet down the dock's worn 2x4 wooden ladder and boarded my first cannery tender.

I was immediately struck with the impression of power and strength that a craft such as this displayed. There was something of a "fortress" about this floating machine. The low bulwarks circling from the fore deck aft around the transom was immensely heavy and crowned with an ironbark toe rail a foot wide and as strong as steel. Her house was pure white, and she was painted orange from toe rail to rub rail. Below the rub rail, the hull was a deep, rich forest green down to the copper paint at the waterline. On each side, she was guarded by five heavy manila fenders, a foot in diameter and woven with care by some artisan whose skills are now beyond recall. They rested on the graying, teak-faced rub rail which was wide enough to stand on.

The deck was heavily planked and cambered to shed on-board seas, as unyielding to the feet as if someone were walking on bed-rock. A raised portion of decking crossed the stern, holding a huge manila tow line nearly three inches in diameter. It seemed impossible to me that anyone would ever need a rope that big. Bolted to the deck, just aft of the main deckhouse, was the massive cast-iron towing bit that weighed at least a ton or more. The steel through-bolts used to hold it down were as big as my arm, larger than any bolt I had ever seen before. Everything about her spoke of strength and utility.

The *Doris* had a two-story house with the wheel house rather forward on the second deck, in much the same manner as a conventional tug boat. Cannery tenders of the day were of two main types. There were those which carried fish on board in holds designated for the purpose and those, more refined, which served as tow boats and packed fish in barges carried alongside or towed astern. The *Doris* was strictly a towboat. She carried too much dignity to be sullied with the ever present odor of a vessel with a fish hold. Secured to the aft end of the deckhouse, just above and to the left of the towbit, was a food locker equipped with a couple of perforated doors. Dried blood had congealed on its bottom and sides. I would learn later it could be easily found in the dark if one followed the smell of old meat. Next to the food locker a small clothes line held the only signs of life on board, two drying dish towels and a pair of mottled gray socks, nee white.

I started to walk forward toward the bow when an ancient face suddenly appeared from a varnished doorway, and exploded in a gruff voice, "Hey kid what the hell do you want here?" The authoritative face, crowned by a soiled white hat, belonged to Fred Foster, poet laureate and cook on the *Doris E.* I mumbled something about being the son of the Superintendent and that, "I just wanted to look around the boat." He ordered me into the galley, directing my way by gesturing with a dripping potato-masher. For a few moments he just wheezed and looked me over as if he were examining some kind of plant life. He looked like the oldest man I had ever seen. I had invaded his territory and the territory of five other men. I had not requested permission to come aboard, and I believe he was convinced I had no damn business there in the first place. Furthermore, I sat now in his galley, a place where he was obviously the Lord and Master and now in complete control of my fate.

He devoted the next few minutes to a rather lengthy questioning about where I'd come from, what was my name, when had I arrived at the cannery, and why was I sneaking around on his boat? Somewhat confused he growled, "Hell, I didn't even know the old man had a kid." I explained that my mother and step-father had just been married in Juneau and that we were going to stay at the cannery a couple of weeks until the steamer came back. He turned back to the stove and abused something in the bottom of a pot with his potato masher. A minute later he softened a little and uncovered a large plate of doughnuts, indicating I should try one.

As he continued his questions and resumed his cooking activities, I had the opportunity to get a good look at my host. He was indeed a very old man, and the years had bent him forward from the waist up. This particular morning he sported a short gray stubble that needed shaving. I was to learn that shaving was not one of his major concerns. When he moved, he hobbled about the galley, speaking sometimes to me and sometimes to himself. He was constantly wiping up non-existent spills or crumbs with an off-white cloth that never left his right hand no matter what else he carried. The trousers beneath his stained apron drooped down and almost totally obscured his deck shoes, the toes of which bore small stains of various condiments and sauces.

Fred's glasses were the kind you tried out in Woolworth's then bought for two-bits. I knew that because my grandfather wore the same kind. I was to learn there was another constant about Fred Foster; he always smelled of Sloan's liniment; it wasn't unpleasant, it was just always about him, and about the galley. It was a hospital kind of smell. At age 82, he was miraculously playing a young man's game, Sloan's liniment was the oil that kept his body moving. After a while you never noticed it.

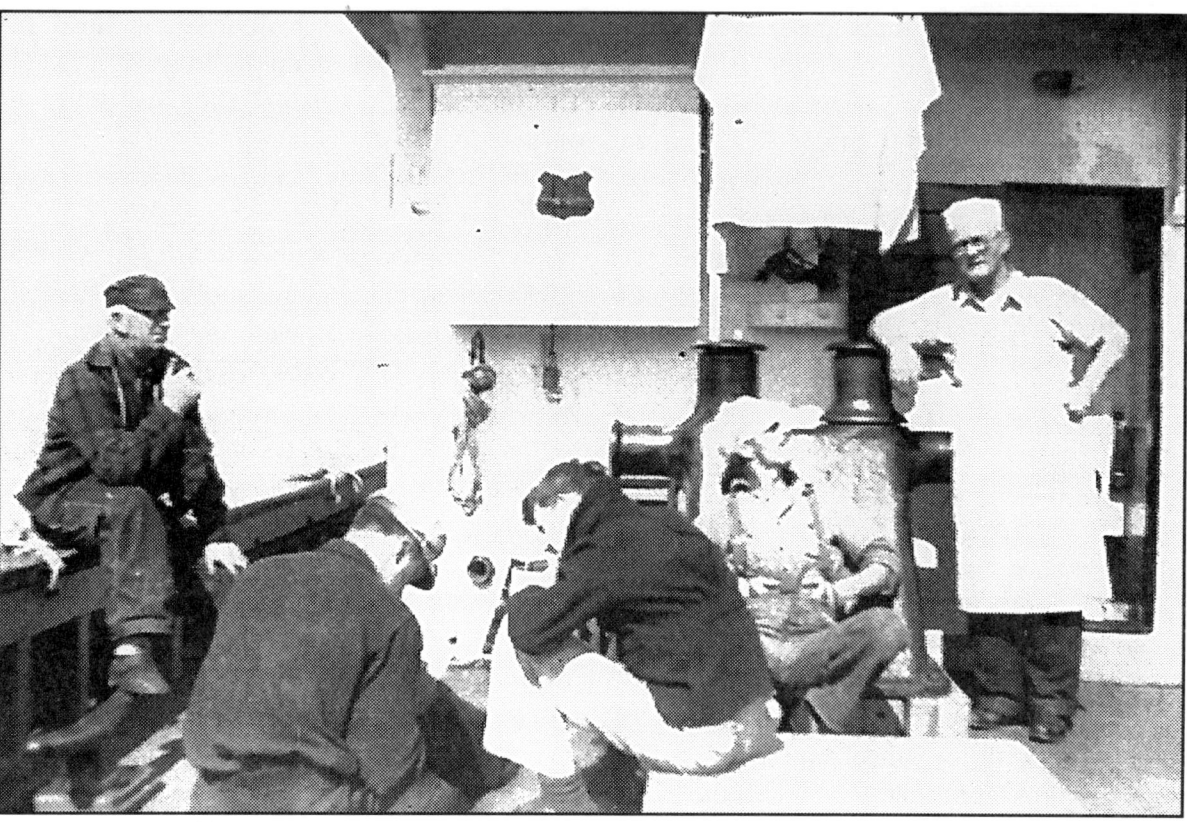

The back deck of the *Doris E*. From left to right, Claude Graham the Engineer smokes a pipe on the rail. Second Engineer Kato Schwalling and the author sit on the aft hatch. Phil Hastin, the Mate, lounges against the tow bit, while Fred Foster, the Cook, supervises the leisure activities.

No matter what the size or state of dilapidation, the galley was the social hall of every work vessel I ever boarded. The *Doris* was no exception. The galley on the *Doris* ran athwartships, that is side to side across the boat in the forward portion of the main deckhouse. It was perhaps fourteen feet wide by twelve feet fore and aft, an immense space on a tow boat. A great deal of this area was taken up by a kidney shaped table at the forward side of the room on which the crew sat in an inviolate pecking order on a long curved bench. The table was totally bordered by a strip of polished oak extending up from the top surface about an inch. This raised ledge kept the dishes from sliding off the table in heavy weather. The surface of the table was a reddish linoleum which was seldom seen. The minute the boat was underway, Fred Foster covered the surface with a large dampened table cloth cut to fit the table's exact curved outline. This damp but ingenious addition kept plates, saucers, cups and cutlery from sliding around or upsetting except when the weather got particularly nasty. Tall condiments like Ketchup, Worcestershire Sauce, Tabasco and salt and pepper were neatly contained in a roll-proof oak box on the forward edge of the table.

The heavier the weather, the wetter the cloth. In a real storm the crew ate "cold stuff" while standing up; if it were bad enough, they didn't eat at all.

The galley of the *Doris* was a light and pleasant place. In addition to the "Dutch" doors on each side, there were two large square windows in each of the port and starboard bulkheads. Doors to the galley were bottomed with high thresholds, perhaps nine inches above the deck, to keep out sea water which might come aboard. The forward bulkhead was fitted with thick port lights to withstand any green water which might roll over the bow. This occurred quite frequently. Fred Foster always kept the top portions of the doors latched open, they were his windows on the world. Periodically he would hobble to either side, peek out, and comment on the passing scene, to himself or to whomever might be listening. It was a ritual I would get to enjoy over the treasured time I spent with him.

The aft bulkhead of the galley was fitted with various cupboards and built in drawers. All were designed to securely hold plates, cups and other needed cooking implements. Large pots and frying pans hung from hooks on the bulkhead, making worn little arcs where they had swung back and forth through the years. To preclude spillage, drawers had to be lifted slightly to be opened. Inside, there was a place for each and every item. On the port side of the aft bulkhead sat a heavy cast iron "Shipmate" stove which was diesel-fired and

Left to right, Kato Schwalling on deck, the author and Skipper Norman Hodgson on the bridge

always warm. Projections rising from the top corners of the cooking surface served as holders for pieces of notched iron bar which could be placed at various points and angles to keep pots and pans securely in place in a rough sea. A small, adjustable electric blower maintained a controlled heat in the oven or on top of the stove. It also warmed the galley in any kind of weather. Everything in sight was immaculate and in order, it was one of Fred Foster's compulsions, a way of life.

The predominant "feel" of the galley could best be described as secure and comfortable, a little like my grandmother's kitchen. The cannery tenders were painted from stem to stern every spring

37

in Seattle before heading north for Alaska. Thus the bulkheads on the *Doris E* were covered by myriad coats of gleaming white enamel creating the effect of a deep pool of brilliance. She had worked hard all season and she was beginning to show a few chinks in her armor. Here and there a scratch or scuff intruded, but the subtlety of her colors and textures were still wonderful. In contrast to the gloss of the bulkheads, the surfaces of cabinets, tables and benches, all in oak or straight grain fir or pine, gleamed with coat after coat of hard spar varnish, a transparent medium extolling the beauty of their distinctive textures. The gold sheen of brass screws added to the beauty. The deck was covered with heavy battleship linoleum, annually painted a rich red-brown, and softened to a velvet patina by constant sweeping. The stove contributed to the color array with an accent of heavy flat black that was complemented by the gleam of copper bottomed pans and the shine of heavy white tableware. There was a richness here which pronounced this spot to be far more than just a place to eat. It was a dining lounge, a Great Hall and a sanctuary where everyone belonged.

My mother and dad felt I was too young to drink coffee, but this special morning when Fred Foster offered me a cup, I didn't refuse. I wanted to belong at this table. The coffee was served black and red-hot from a huge enameled pot kept on the back of the stove. From habit he braced himself against the table edge as if we were in a heavy roll, and poured the molten liquid into a thick white mug that was almost too heavy to lift. I laced it with sugar and the "canned cow" from the oak box on the table and answered some more questions. Fred named the other crew members and allowed as, "He didn't know how the hell they'd take to a kid even visiting aboard, and that they'd still keep cussin' if they goddam well wanted to even if the old man's kid was hanging around!" I was finding it a little hard to fit in, but I gave it a try. I think I said something like, "That was sure as hell OK with me." He gave me a look indicating that I should clean up my mouth. I slunk down a little behind the coffee cup and didn't cuss anymore.

There was noise on deck and a small, agile man in a red mackinaw and white cap stepped into the galley through the port doorway. He smiled and looked a little surprised as he and Fred exchanged glances. Fred waved a large spoon which had replaced the masher and told him I was the Superintendent's kid. With a grin a foot wide he stuck out his hand and asked me my name. For the first time I met Phil Hastin, first mate of the *Doris E*, and one of the great men I've known in my life. That initial meeting has stretched into friendship of nearly sixty years. For the next three summers Phil Hastin, only ten years my senior, taught me lessons everyone has to learn. There should be a man like that in every kid's life. The next year, at the age of twenty-four, he became the youngest skipper of the fleet. My dad gave him his first command, an ancient rust bucket called the *Eagle*. He transformed the old tub into a bona-fide tug boat. No one ever deserved a command more, or handled it better.

There were four more crewmen of the *Doris* who were to become my treasured friends. In a situation that can only be described as unique, each one extended to me a kindness and sensitivity which affected my life. A group of hard-bitten sailors can hardly be expected to identify with the needs of an adolescent kid. In this case they did. Their acceptance of me as a token member of their group was the kind of happenstance that every adolescent boy dreams of. On the *Doris* the dream became reality.

Norman Hodgson was skipper of the *Doris E*. He was a tough, gregarious, heavy-set man who was always gruff with me and always caring. He had no problem dealing with his crew and his leadership was derived from the respect of the men around him. The years have distilled an essence of memories about these men I lived and worked with as a child. That distillation is perhaps more meaningful and more real than if they were sitting beside me today. It's impossible for me to picture Norman Hodgson without a tough smile, a barking voice and a pair of suspenders— I mean huge suspenders, gray and blue striped, with great chrome fittings that snapped down on heavy elastic straps a full two inches wide. Most of the boat crews wore suspenders, but with Hodgson they seemed a part of his being. When I was on his boat, Hodgson treated me as a man, not a child. He created a role for me and I did my best to fulfill it.

When Norman Hodgson shouted orders from the wheelhouse window, it set the on-shore ravens to flight. Everyone within earshot jumped to obey. Later on, when I spent more time on the boat, my passage aboard was always paid with a Mozart cigar taken from a box kept in my Dad's desk. As I'd start down the boarding ladder Hodgson would shout, "Hey Eddie, you got that cigar?" He would light it immediately drawing in great draughts of the gray smoke and exclaim, "God, I wish I could afford these like your old man," It became a ritual. My dad always kept the Mozarts in supply and Hodgson never eased up on the demand. I learned later that a deal had been struck between the two and that I was only the instrument that effected the exchange. The Mozarts were payment for services rendered. If the skipper was to watch over the boss's kid, a good smoke was deemed to be just compensation.

Claude Graham was Chief Engineer. He was quiet and a seemingly ancient being, who said little and knew every nut and bolt of the *Doris's* engine. Typically, he wore a small, black, short-visored engineer's cap and smoked a pipe that looked like it had been stolen from Sherlock Holmes. I knew nothing of his family or his background; he was a private person, soft spoken yet friendly. Much of what I know of diesel engines I learned from Claude shouting in my ear in the confines of the clatter and roar of his engine room on the *Doris E*.

Kato Schwalling, the Second Engineer was a tall, spare, good looking kid who was always joking and continually moving. Kato was probably eighteen or nineteen in those early days on the *Doris*. With Bud Iversen, the deckhand, we three would constitute the "kid faction" of the *Doris E*. In the years ahead I was influenced by each of these men in a different fashion, Every man aboard contributed to a period of my life that was deep in the richness of growing up. The security and pride of belonging to a boat and its crew and sharing the daily adventure of life in a rigorous, exciting and primitive land was a miraculous opportunity that filled those days with wonder and my future years with treasured memories.

Bud Iversen left and Kato Schwalling right. Kato died at Bataan.

When Fred Foster was through with his interrogation, I asked for and got an OK to explore the boat with which I would identify for the rest of my life. The bow of the *Doris E* bore a massive stem iron looking very much like a section of heavy railroad track. The bow was raked just slightly forward in typical towboat style. The top of the stem iron was crowned with an eye bolt fitting to which was anchored the forestay that ran upward to the mast head. Massive chain plates were bolted to the bulwarks on either side of the mast to which the shrouds were made fast. A ratline or ladder ran up the shrouds on the starboard side only. I climbed it only once. Seeing me at the top, Norm Hodgson told me to, "get the hell down from there or he'd break my goddam neck!" The statement seemed rather redundant, a fact I chose not to mention at the time.

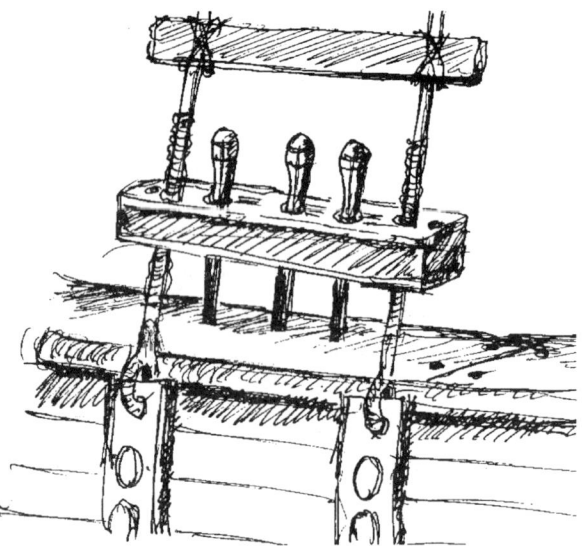

The foredeck on the *Doris* was raised about two feet above the main deck to provide additional forecastle headroom. A Samson post twelve inches square was mounted just aft of the bow for belaying forward tow lines, and a combination anchor and lifting winch beginning to show summer's rust, was mounted just aft of the post. The winch was equipped with two heads, one for cable, and the other with a sprocket surface to lift the six inch links of the anchor chain. The winch was huge and operated from a geared-down electric motor which always spun in a weird monotone. Control of the cable lifting head was accomplished through a friction clutch and a common foot-pedal brake. Claude Graham was the sole operator of the winch. I recall him bathed in noise, standing like a stork with a raised foot on the winch brake pedal and a dirty hand wrapped around the cold steel of the winch handle. His touch was light, delicate, and essential to the safety of all aboard; there was never an error in lifting or lowering no matter what the load or how bad the weather.

The mast was stepped perhaps eight to ten feet forward of the deckhouse. It was about twelve to fourteen inches in diameter and stepped through the deck and the forecastle to the keel. It extended about fifty-five feet above the deck. The boom, slightly less in diameter, extended about ten feet higher then the mast. Both spars were of beautiful straight grain spruce. A heavy manila topping lift connected the end of the boom to an eye band about five feet down from the head of the mainmast, and all this constituted the lifting gear essential to cannery tender operation.

The forecastle head was located just abaft the mast on the starboard side. Six or eight worn, wooden steps led down into a gloomy interior. On both port and starboard bulkheads, three heavy brass port lights admitted an amount of light equivalent to that found at the bottom of a mine shaft. In order to see down there one pulled on a dirty string that was attached to an ugly bare bulb hanging from the overhead. Two sets of upper and lower bunks lined the port and starboard bulkheads. These bunks served extra temporary crewmen during the fishing season. The forecastle sole, a rich copper-red, slanted slightly upward toward the forepeak, and a forward bulkhead provided the compartment for an anchor chain locker. There was always the smell of a stale sea blanketing the forecastle. When the anchor was lifted the chain deposited a couple of gallons of salt water and kelp fragments in the chain locker. In a few days this mini-aquarium festered and made itself known throughout the confines of the forecastle. Although the sea smell was quite strong, it wasn't nearly as bad as that arising from the pair of old socks and long underwear that I noticed that morning abandoned damp and unwashed in the corner of an upper bunk. The chain locker bulkhead was festooned with a couple of girlie calendar photographs from a garage in Seattle. At my age, such visual experiences were beginning to intrigue me.

Visible in the overhead was the strength of the vessel. Huge 8x8 inch cambered timbers ran athwartships every two feet supporting the foredeck. The bulkheads and overhead were painted a brilliant white which sparkled in the light of the single globe. A ledge of straight grained oak extended the length of each bunk about two inches above the height of the mattress. It was specifically designed to keep a sleeping body from rolling off the bunk in heavy weather, a situation which could otherwise easily occur. The mattresses were of the "no fluff" variety, covered with blue and white ticking, and seemingly stuffed with straw. I can only judge them to have been adequate, since I never suffered from lack of sleep. Lower bunks were faced with large varnished drawers bearing brass pulls where the crew stored clothing, dirty magazines, illicit booze and other personal effects.

The mast was a massive white pillar transfixing the interior of the cabin like a giant sword. It extended down through the sole and into the keel and gave the forecastle an air of immense strength and rigidity. A mirrored medicine chest was affixed to the forward portion of the mast just above a small wash basin equipped with bronze hot and cold water faucets. The mirror was always dirty, always spotted with dried toothpaste, and the water was always cold. Just aft of the mast, against the rear bulkhead, a small coal/wood stove was bolted to the floor, and beside it was a small wood bin. I never saw it used. If one was off watch and it was cold, it was much more effective to crawl beneath the covers than to trouble oneself by building a fire.

The mirror was always dirty...the water was always cold.

The wheelhouse on the *Doris* perched forward on the second deck and echoed the gleaming white and warm shining wood of the rest of the vessel. A walkway boarded with an iron railing circled the front and sides of the wheelhouse allowing the skipper to exit the cabin and see fore and aft. Three large windows were set in the forward bulkhead and offered excellent visibility. The windows could be opened by lowering them into a pocket in the bulkhead by way of a thick leather belt and they could be raised by the same belt and pushed into a detent which kept them closed. A giant traditional ship's wheel, perhaps four feet in diameter, was mounted forward just aft of a wide shelf running athwartships. The shelf was of sufficient width to hold a dinner plate, several coffee cups, or a round of beers provided the time was appropriate. It also held cigar stubs, old salmon lures, yesterdays socks and copies of Norwegian newspapers which I was never able to decipher.

Immediately behind the wheel on the same shaft was a gear and chain which led down through the wheelhouse sole to the mechanics of a primitive automatic pilot, always referred to as "Iron Mike." At times it worked and at other times it produced a zig-zag course which would have done credit to a frightened rabbit. The compass was large, dull black enameled, and lit by a traditional red binnacle light which reflected at night like a ruby against the cold pane of the center window. It was gimbaled to maintain a semblance of being level in heavy weather and regulated by two large cast iron balls perhaps three or four inches in diameter bolted to brackets on either side of the swinging face. I remember it now, as it was on many a night, a tiny island of light in a world of pervasive darkness and storm. There was a symbolism there for one who wished to pursue it.

To the right of the wheel, two rods ran up through the wheelhouse sole and were topped by two solid brass levers about two feet in length. These were the engine controls. They operated in a large horizontal arc. One lever controlled the governor thus setting the speed of the engine. The other lever operated a massive air-assisted clutch changing the propeller rotation from ahead to astern or vice-versa. These were not "finger-food" operating levers; they were heavy brass castings keyed into inch and a half steel rods. They were moved by using all the muscles in your arm, not by the flick of a wrist. The ends of the actuating levers were cast into classical handle forms which had been polished to a velvet smoothness through years of use.

Wheelhouse controls were not the usual fare on cannery tenders. In most vessels, bell signals were sent to an engineer standing by during maneuvering or docking. He, in turn, operated the clutch and governor speed as directed by the bells from the wheelhouse. In the engine room of the *Doris E*, the effect of going from ahead to astern was dramatic. Every movement of the clutch control was accompanied by a tremendous blast of high-pressure air. There followed an absolute symphony of sound as huge drums and levers changed positions and meshed, first slowing, then reversing the rotation of the mammoth tail shaft. It was exciting, and the action so monumental one might think that God himself was pulling the levers on the bridge.

If one sat while steering, it was on a high oak stool whose legs were cross-wired at the bottom and which appeared as old as Noah's Ark. The leather seat was padded and encircled by brass tacks with rounded heads. I loved to place my feet on the two lower spokes of the wheel and tilt the stool back slightly. Hours of sea dreams were passed this way. When Norm Hodgson was on the bridge, I steered standing up "Like any goddam deckhand ought to do."

A single built-in bunk for "cat nap" use by the skipper lined the aft bulkhead of the wheelhouse. Hodgson used it when the *Doris E* was underway at night or in close passages. After a nap of minutes he would arise and peer carefully through the windows, orienting himself and making sure that all was well. He would then return to his bunk without a word. I wondered at times if he had really awakened at all. His action was akin to the behavior of a sleeping cat, resting, wary, and vigilant. A change of five RPM in engine speed would awaken him in an instant and, should the situation demand, he could be fully awake at the wheel in less than two seconds.

Mounted above the bunk was the huge black box of the radio. It was state of the art and about two and a half feet square with lots of static and a very short range. When Norman Hodgson used the radio, he screamed into the microphone so loudly that most of us thought his voice carried directly through the air to the intended recipient. The transmitter was probably only for "show." The *Doris* was one of only a very few tenders equipped with radios. A daily radio schedule between the *Doris* and the cannery was attempted, but not always accomplished due to the vagaries of weather, location, and equipment. Screwed to the aft bulkhead next to the radio, was a fine Seth Thomas striking clock and a companion barometer which was always tapped gently with a forefinger before being believed. From the overhead the heavy brass handle of an adjustable searchlight extended down perhaps a foot, just short of being a "head-banger."

Next to the searchlight handle hung the lanyard for the air horn. It was beautifully finished off with a "Turk's Head" of fancy knotting which was dirtied by years of use. The air horn lacked all the romance of a steam whistle, maintaining just enough nautical authenticity to be acceptable. On the starboard bulkhead hung an ancient foghorn, a slim brass funnel, perhaps two feet long ending in a five inch bell. The business end of the horn was placed in one's mouth and blown in foggy weather and at such other times as were judged appropriate. The mouthpiece of the thing was made of wood and always tasted bad. In the years to come, I was directed on many occasions to assume the responsibility for blowing this horn. Another duty was involved. Foggy or clear, Norm Hodgson would demand that I keep the horn shiny and sparkling with a combination of *Brilliant Shine* paste and hours of vigorous massage.

On the port side, there were three staterooms aft of the galley. The one forward was occupied by Norm Hodgson and Phil Hastin. The next cabin aft could be instantly identified by the smell of Sloan's Liniment and belonged to Fred Foster. The third cabin aft was designated as the Superintendent's cabin and was usually full of sacks of flour, sugar, other staples and cases of canned goods. They used the space for storage since Dad didn't make many overnight runs on the tenders. On the starboard side were an additional two cabins. The one forward was occupied by Claude Graham and his assistant engineer, Kato Schwalling. Bud Iversen, the deckhand slept in the aft cabin. All the cabins had wash basins and there was a "head" located on the starboard side, which was flushed by vigorously pumping an oak handle about two feet long. Doors to the cabins were located about eighteen inches above the deck and entrance was made by way of an intermediate teak step. The solid mahogany cabin doors were bordered with grab-rails on the outside and the door hardware was massive cast brass. A small storage hatch was situated perhaps five feet aft of the deckhouse.

If one passed through a doorway on the starboard side of the aft end of the deckhouse and descended six or eight steps down a heavy wooden staircase, he would find himself in the engine room, the heart of the *Doris E*. It was a large compartment, about thirty feet long and beam to beam wide. The engine, a colossal Washington Estep Diesel of one hundred and eighty horsepower, was one of the most beautiful and impressive machines I have ever seen. The engine assembly, with its huge clutch, was perhaps fourteen to sixteen feet long, and each of the four mammoth cylinders was two feet in diameter and towered to more than seven feet high. An

The massive engine room was the domain of Claude Graham, Chief Engineer. The Washington Estep diesel engine was the most impressive machine I had ever seen.

immense flywheel was mounted on the front end of the engine. It was five feet in diameter and at least eight inches across weighing probably a ton or more. Such huge flywheels, with their accompanying inertia, smoothed out the running and vibration of these slow speed diesels. The flywheel was so large, it required a two foot well cut into the engine room floor to accommodate its rotation. The floor or sole was the same rust red color as that found in the galley, for the simple reason that a can of such color had probably already been opened.

The engine room bulkheads were brilliant white. A large bench and tool board lined the starboard side of the engine room. An air compressor and rectangular air tank were situated just forward of the bench which was painted white and bore a large vise on the aft end. The tool board was traditionally marked with painted outlines indicating exactly where specific tools belonged. I recall borrowing a hammer once to pound out a bent fish hook. Typically, I failed to return it immediately. Dictated by Claude Graham, punishment for this transgression consisted of a complete wipe down and cleaning of the tool board and the engine room sole. I didn't forget again.

As I recall, the Washington Estep Diesel was the result of a design created by Dr. Estep, a professor of Mechanical Engineering at the University of Washington. Actual production was accomplished by the Washington Iron Works located, I believe, in South Seattle. I would calculate the weight of the *Doris's* engine to be about 20,000 to 30,000 pounds. For anyone who loved engines, this massive creation was a triumph of form, color, and texture; more important, it could pull like hell! There was a romance and life in these huge engines. Working parts moved and pounded before you creating an indelible, wondrous sound. After starting them men always smiled, like children with an electric train. Some time ago I wrote:

I recall the huge injectors were about eighteen inches long and machined to perfection, sculptures in brass and steel. The in-

jector lines were like hard, gold necklaces. The valve springs were black and massive, with silver push rods about four feet long contrasting beautifully against the forest green of the engine.

I can draw her picture, but I can't draw her voice. There was the rush of compressed air...then the first ignition...the birth of firing...the clatter of push rods and valves, and then the smell and sound of raw, sweet, power. I'll never forget it.

This then, was the vessel with which I have identified all my life. I am looking at a sepia-toned photograph of the *Doris E* taken half a century ago. She lies moored to a floating salmon trap frame, and I believe I can see the figure of Fred Foster bustling in the galley. It is probably lunch time. Just aft of the wheelhouse, on the second deck, a massive stack rises four feet above the top of the wheelhouse and bears the logo of the Alaska Pacific Salmon Co. Just aft of the stack and slung in davits are two nested dories which saw constant use. Aft of the dories and at the end of the deckhouse rises a 20 foot flagpole which, at times, bore a flag of 48 stars. Her shrouds, topping lift, forestay, and hoisting cable are silhouetted against a gray sky that promises rain, but the galley would be warm and the coffee would be hot on the back burner. Most important, I could catch fifteen giant rock cod off her fantail on one change of tide. It was a life-style to be envied and admired.

We had been at Port Althorp for a week when my Dad came home early one afternoon. My mother was in the kitchen and I was reading *Pacific Fisherman*. It was obvious that something was wrong. Word had come over the radio that the purse seiner *Eidsvold* was missing. She had been fishing "outside" off the West Coast of Prince of Wales Island. The *Eidsvold* had sent a radio message that she had hit a big run of fish off Dall Island and they had filled the boat with a deck load of salmon. In addition and, in what would have been a tricky procedure, they were also towing a loaded seine net filled with fish. The weather had "kicked up a little," and they were on their way in. No one ever saw or heard from her again. Two weeks later a crushed skiff washed ashore with a life jacket caught on an oarlock. She had gone down with all hands. Aboard her was Frederick Peter Buschmann, the second son of Eigel and Nora. Fred was just twenty-one and, by all accounts his mother's favorite.

Other Boats, Other Engines.

At my age I saw her skipper as an old man. He was about fifty at the time, he rarely shaved and drank coffee from a cup that bore the stains of ages of unwashed droolings.

In the depression years, men fished with boats like this and worse. With hard work they could earn enough to buy beer, booze or a Bachelors degree...Which they chose, dictated the direction of their lives.

As I have stated before, I am convinced that boats are living breathing entities that possess unique traits of their own...some good, some bad. The cannery tenders of Port Althorp were no exception. The cannery was served by five cannery tenders of varying ages, appearances, and abilities. The *Doris E* was the biggest and the best. Next in line was the *Sally S,* a pretender to the throne. The *Sally S* was identical to the *Doris,* but with a three cylinder Washington Estep diesel of 165 horsepower, fifteen horsepower less than her sister. They looked like twins but the *Sally's* heart was smaller and she seemed a dilettante, finicky and prim. Significantly, we referred to her as the "Silly Ass." Even her crew was different, aloof and somewhat combative. I didn't care that much for the *Sally*.

The *Service* was a run-of-the-mill tender, gasoline powered, squatty, and about 75 feet in length. She had a midship deckhouse and a cook who constantly expounded from the Bible and quoted psalms from morning to night. Mixed with the culinary offerings, were ongoing attempts at "soul saving," and the galley seemed much like the narthex of a Baptist Church. Without cussing and talk about sex, there wasn't that much to learn. It wasn't much fun aboard her either, and I spent little time there. The *Service* was a "pedestrian boat," doing her job and lacking the shine and excitement of imminent adventure. I have known girls like her, capable in the kitchen but out of the question as dates for the Senior Prom.

The *Lloyd C* was a much older, rather decrepit boat, seemingly arthritic and about 70 feet in length. She would never stand out in a crowd. She was diesel powered, and I recall her exhaust manifold was covered with a tattered wrapping of white asbestos which hung down like uncombed hair. It needed trimming or repairs which could have been effected with a pair of scissors. It is significant that the repairs never happened. She lacked agility and, in the course of a long career, had bumped into too many things, leaving her rub rails dented and badly used. In spite of her masculine name, she had the appearance of an older woman, jaded, with make-up badly applied, and one who might sell her wares on the corner were anyone willing to buy. The *Lloyd C* was a vessel to be tolerated, not loved.

The *Hero* was something else. She was smaller still, perhaps 65 feet long and bright and lively. She had recently been the proud recipient of a new Atlas Imperial diesel engine of 110 horsepower, a gleaming jewel of an engine which started with gentle breaths of compressed air, and ran like a sewing machine. She was a clean little boat, able and agile and moved quickly about her work. Her skipper ran a tight ship and carved beautiful little sailboats from pieces of yellow pine. The *Hero* exuded a feeling of youth in the way she looked and in the way she worked. She had good "sea lines," and her bow wave was always nice and clean and white—I liked this boat.

The *Eagle* stood at the bottom of the pecking order. She was an aged craft often referred to as the "Slab," which next year would be Phil Hastin's first command. At my age, I saw her skipper as an old man. He was about fifty at the time, rarely shaved, and drank coffee from a cup that bore the stains of ages of unwashed droolings. Smaller even than the *Hero*, the *Eagle* was powered by a Standard gasoline engine which smoked even when it was turned off, and emitted fifty questionable horsepower. From a short distance, the engine looked like a misshapen lump of rust. Smaller parts had melted into the reddish coating of corrosion and were indistinguishable. Even the spark plugs were almost impossible to find. White crusty growths covered the battery cables, belts were loose, and empty cans of lubricating oil lay among her frame timbers.

The engine sat in a "bilge of horrors" in which things floated and from which strange odors arose. A rumor abounded that some of her crew pissed in the bilge rather than undertake the long trek to the head which was located at the rear of the deckhouse. It was also rumored that this practice was even more prevalent during the course of heavy and persistent rains. I believe this to be true. The practice was stopped the following year when Phil Hastin became skipper and promised to knock hell out of anybody substituting the bilge for the head. The *Eagle* always smelled better after that.

With all her shortcomings, the *Eagle* had a soul of majestic proportions. Although the contrast was enormous, next to the *Doris* I liked her the best. She was a boat to be defended not scorned. I took exception to the many instances when slurs and remarks were made about her. I saw something of a "David" about the *Eagle*, particularly when she was wrestling some large scow against an overpowering tide. Phil and the *Eagle* were invincible, more than the sum of their parts. From some inner well of strength they gathered

the will to do the job of a boat twice her size. When she was moored, I always had the feeling that because she was old, she was resting and saving her strength for the next series of miracles she would be called upon to perform. I don't know where she is now, but her soul can rest in pride. She was a hell of a towboat. Phil Hastin, her skipper, handled her beautifully and she was easy to love and admire.

Fishing vessels were the working tools of the men who drew their living from the sea. They came in all shapes and sizes, their form being classically derived from their function. If cannery tenders and towboats were of the highest order in the marine vessel "food chain," the small skiffs and dories of the hand trollers were the lowest form of life. In the closing years of the thirties the depression had eased and things were looking better, but a dollar was still a very important commodity. In 1938, 39, and 40 I met men who would set sail on a one by twelve if they thought they might catch a few salmon and make a few bucks.

Hand trollers had to be a hardy lot. Their vessels ranged from polished New England dories to motley skiffs which required constant bailing. Some had outboards which were always hidden in a mist of oil smoke; others rowed their craft with a classic ease and economy of motion. In their yellow oilskins and Sou'wester hats, the rowers seemed a part of the waters they fished, primeval, like something out of a painting by Winslow Homer. They fished "inside," of course where the weather was flatter and better, but they fished without shelter in driving rains and winds that would discourage any person of sound mind and body. And, they made money. With many, their earnings went for beer, booze, and ladies, but a few saved their hard-earned gains and moved on to better and bigger boats and a brighter and better future. They were the men who had learned a great and pervasive truth often quoted by my dad, "You can't catch fish at the dock."

If one worked and learned, the next step up was a small powered trolling boat. These also came in all shapes and sizes. In the years I spent in Alaska, the classic trolling boat was perhaps twenty five to thirty five feet in length, gasoline powered, with a trunk cabin providing a small bunk, stove, and shelter for the fisherman and the engine. These boats were of classic design. Many of the hulls were copies of the sailing felluccas which plied the seas of the Middle East before the time of Christ. Power was supplied by primitive gasoline engines with antique ignition systems and large flywheels which were turned by hand for starting. Many of these engines were produced by the Hicks or Frisco Standard Companies, located in San Francisco, or the Atlas Gas Engine Company of Oakland, California. They were cranky and turned so slowly it was easy to count the power strokes they produced. If one slowly repeats the word Po-ta-to, Po-ta-to, Po-ta-to, it approximates the sound of the early Hicks Engine.

These marine engines were heavy, massive in size, and required constant manual lubrication. Castings were often ornate and sometimes embellished with relief representations of leaves or flowers by some poetic foundry worker. I found this practice to be fascinating, a crying out for beauty in a world of noise and power. Bearings were of primitive babbit metal, hand poured and fitted. The ignition source was a magneto, and the spark was produced by a spring loaded contraption labeled a "make-and-break" spark producer. Sometimes they worked, and many times they did not.

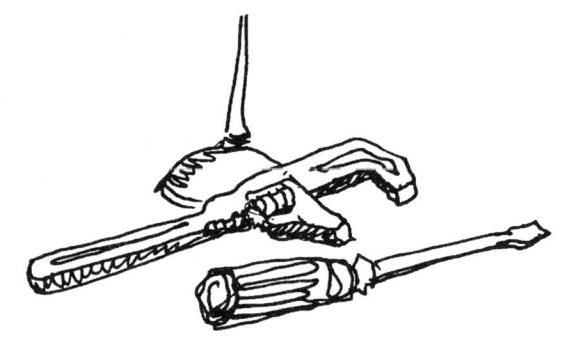

The typical trolling boat mounted two trolling poles forward and two, rather longer, amidships. These trolling poles could be hoisted to the vertical position while the vessel was in transit and lowered to a near-horizontal position when the vessel was fishing thus clearing the lines from the boat's wake. Lines with heavy lead weights and artificial lures or bait were trailed from the trolling poles and were retrieved by the use of engine powered reels or gurdies. During fishing, the boat's speed and direction were controlled and fish were landed while the operator stood waist-high in a "gaff hatch" in the stern of the boat. The term is derived from the act of gaffing or boating the fish by means of a large, heavy, wooden-handled gaff or hook.

The trolling method of fishing was selective in that only two of the five species of salmon were usually caught by this method. Although there were exceptions, King or Chinook Salmon, *(Oncorhynchus tshawytscha)* and Cohos or Silvers, *(Oncorhynchus kisutch)* were the species usually caught while trolling. Both of these species are highly prized. Fish were kept in a small fish hold just forward of the gaff hatch until delivered to a cannery. Some of these trolling boats were maintained in "Bristol" or prime condition by their owners, and some were so unsightly they defied description. Actually anything that floated would do. The size of the catch depended upon the knowledge, tenacity, and skill of the fisherman, and the good fortune to be in the right place at the right time.

A unique type of fishing vessel was used in the shallow waters of Bristol Bay, Alaska. I had no personal experience with these boats, but they were classic craft surely worthy of inclusion in any discussion of Alaskan fishing boats. These Bristol Bay gill net boats were strictly sailing craft since engines were legally prohibited in the Bristol Bay area in the 1920's, 30's, and 40's. Gill net boats were about thirty feet in length and completely open save for a small sheltered area in the bow. The hulls were classic Mid-eastern, felucca-style, adhering to the age old designs of Mediterranean fishing vessels. The mast was stepped well forward with a very long boom and sprit which carried a nearly unilateral triangle sail.

Like many of the trollers, these double-ended gill-net boats had ribs of steamed oak and the best were planked with Port Orford cedar. This oily wood was obtainable only in the vicinity of Port Orford, Oregon, and now, almost unattainable, is arguably the finest hull planking in the world. Properly fastened and cared for, there is practically no limit to the life of a Port Orford cedar hull. After seventy-five years in the water, I have seen them emerge as sound as the day they were built. Gill net craft were fast, tiller-steered, and bore a rather wide coaming around the entire perimeter of the cockpit to shed on-board water. Each was equipped with long, hardwood oars, which was the only motive force other than sail. As the name implies, the nets carried by these vessels caught salmon by trapping their gills in a mesh especially sized for that purpose. These nets fished well in the shallow waters of the Bay, and their aggregate catch was of major importance to the industry.

The life of the gill net fisherman was difficult and demanding. Each boat was manned by a skipper, and a "puller." The two worked in concert, fishing, cooking, eating and living in a completely open boat for up to a week at a time. A small tent set up in the bow provided scant shelter for bedding and cooking which was done on a one burner kerosene stove. The men who manned these craft were always cold, always tired, always hungry and always wet. They returned year after year, perhaps wanting to convince themselves that nothing could be as bad as the experiences of the prior season.

The next step up in the hierarchy of fishing craft was the Alaska Limit Purse Seine Boat. Limited by territorial law to a keel length of fifty feet, these vessels were a generic "staple" of the Alaskan maritime world. They were usually manned by a crew of four or five men. Salmon caught by purse seining and fish traps formed the backbone of the Alaskan fishing industry. As is the case with all fishing craft, the form of the vessel is dictated by its function, and purse seine boats were no exception. The purse seine was a heavy, smaller meshed net, carried on a turntable on the stern of the vessel. The purse seine was about forty feet wide and perhaps twelve hundred feet long. One edge of the seine net was equipped with round cork floats, and the other edge was equipped with lead weights and rings through which a purse line was passed. When deployed, the net thus hung vertically in the water with the weighted edge and the purse line at the bottom, while the top edge bearing the corks floated at the surface.

Seine boat completing a "set" near Port Althorp. Note the seine skiff and flying bridge. In the days when nets were hauled by hand, seining was an exhausting labor.

When a group of fish were spotted, one end of the seine was held by a crewman in a large skiff while the seine boat made a large circle around the school of salmon. When the circle was completed, the purse line was pulled in closing the bottom of the net, thus forming a large bag from which the fish couldn't escape. The purse seine was then pulled back onto the turntable making the enclosure ever smaller until the fish were contained in a small tight mass. A dip net was then employed to lift the fish from the seine into the hold of the purse seine boat. The whole procedure was called a "set." It was an exhausting process. Ten or twelve sets a day could reduce the strongest crew to a state of total exhaustion.

Seine boats were built with a flying bridge, a steering and control station above the deck level wheelhouse. This steering vantage point allowed the skipper of the craft to spot groups of salmon which might show themselves by shadow, or by "finning "on top of the water. When such a group appeared, a set was made. Sometimes a set could fill a boat, and sometimes the labor resulted in a "water haul," which produced nothing but aching backs and disappointment. Most seine boats were skipper-owned and operated. The boat was fished on a share basis after operating expenses were deducted. The skipper and the boat each received a share of the season's profits and each of the crew was awarded a share. Good skippers made money for themselves and for their crew. Inept skippers often didn't make fuel expenses and their crews received nothing for a season's labors.

Most seine boats provided adequate facilities for their small crews. Basic boat designs were almost cast in stone. There was a small foredeck with a single level house, the forward part of which held the wheelhouse and the after portion, a small galley. A flying bridge with wheel and engine controls topped the wheelhouse, and a heavy mast and boom was stepped at the rear bulkhead aft of the galley. The afterdeck was rather spacious and was dominated by the large turntable which held the purse seine net. The fish hold was located just forward of the seine turntable and aft of the engine room. Seine boats were powered by gasoline or diesel engines in the fifty to one hundred horsepower range, and were built "hell for stout!" Many were impeccably kept and some, because of age or neglect, were floating disasters.

The *Eidsvold*, with Frederick Buschmann aboard was not the first seine boat to be tragically lost at sea, nor was it the last. Every season in Alaska saw the demise of trollers or seine boats. Fishing is a dangerous business now and, without modern technology, was a more dangerous business then. Sinkings and deaths were sometimes the fault of the crew, often the result of vessel or engine failure, and at times, the result of vicious weather which could descend on the unwary in a matter of minutes. The game was quite simple to play and the rules were few; he who ended up with the most fish, won. Several good sets could fill a fish hold, and if a deck load were possible, so much the better. In haste or in carelessness, hatch covers were placed loosely over fish holds filled to the brim. A deck load followed, and the freeboard of the vessel was increasingly diminished to the point of danger. Simply stated, a craft so loaded is put in a situation which exceeds its capability to stay afloat.

Overloading was common and dangerous, but there was always the possibility of even more insidious dangers in some of the older craft. In the classic seine boat, the proximity of fish hold and engine room often invited disaster. The integrity of any vessel is dependent upon the security of its bulkheads, particularly the one between the engine room and the fish hold. If the bulkhead is solid, without leaks, no transfer of water can occur between two areas of the hull, thus the potential for sinking or swamping is greatly reduced. If holes are drilled in the bulkheads for the passage of pipes, wires or other equipment, such gear should be run through watertight packing glands or stuffing boxes which insure compartment integrity. In the years of the 20's and 30's because of haste or lack of money, this practice was not always followed. In addition, if the flotation capability of the craft is to be protected, hatch covers must be battened down tightly to preclude water coming on-board and flooding the fish hold. On some seine boats hatch covers were ill fitting and occasionally not even used. In the event of on-board seas, this practice was of course fraught with danger. I am totally unaware of the age or condition of the *Eidsvold*, but a likely scenario can be formulated to explain the tragic loss of the boat and its crew.

The vessel was fishing in open waters just west of Dall Island and north of Cape Muzon. It is an area which I have already described as vicious and unpredictable in the face of any kind of westerly wind. It is likely that the *Eidsvold* turned northeast to run through Meares Passage, the shortest route to the cannery at Waterfall. With the heavy deck load and towing the seine, the craft would be slowed to the point where she might barely be making way. In this situation, she could be almost certainly overtaken from the rear by a following sea. In that event, water would then sweep across the stern, flooding the after deck and, in turn, pour over the hatch coaming into the loaded fish hold. As water entered the hold, it would also flow through any cracks or openings in the bulkhead causing desperate problems in the engine room.

Since the vessel was already heavily overloaded, the increasing weight of on-board water, combined with the weight of the towed seine would drop the transom further, swamping the after part of the craft. In this condition, it is elementary to conclude that either she simply sank by the stern; or with the loss of longitudinal stability due to a shifting load, rolled quickly to port or starboard, capsized, and went down.

Conjecture is an easy game for one not involved, and facts like these are of little or no import when contrasted with the loss of a young crew striving for a future which would elude them forever. It seems dispassionate and presumptive to attempt to reconstruct the details of the loss of the *Eidsvold*. Frederick's death was a staggering blow to his family and to other people I cared about. Perhaps the "factualization" of the accident somehow reduces the pain I saw in the eyes of those who were most affected. I only know the accident occurred over fifty-five years ago, and I still identify with the loss.

Several weeks had elapsed since we had first landed at Port Althorp, and the northerly winds blowing down from Cape Fairweather had gotten increasingly colder. The cannery tenders had towed the salmon traps to the broad tide flat at the head of the bay, and they were moored safely there until the next spring. Like birds, with their work completed, the cannery tenders, one by one, headed south for Seattle. As I recall, the *Doris* was among the last to leave.

I took a last trip up the pipeline to the dam and fired my .22 rifle a few times. The frost of coming winter crossed the meadows, making them white till midday. Only one person would remain at the cannery through the dark, lonely, winter. An ancient cable splicer named John, who lusted for solitude, would patrol the cannery premises from October till May. With only a radio for company, he would watch from his room in the bunkhouse as deer and an occasional Brown bear would search for scraps of food on the snow covered docks we left behind. The *North Sea* arrived one afternoon to load the last of the canned salmon and to take the last of the crew south for the winter. My mother, dad, and I made the trip back to Seattle, subdued and saddened by the loss of the *Eidsvold* and Frederick Buschmann.

Winter...and the Season of '39

At the fantail, a welter of white and green water leaps upward and spreads across the surface as the six-foot propeller picks up speed and the vessel "hunkers down" for a better pull.

The rains of early fall welcomed us back to Seattle. The trip south had been relatively flat even across Dixon Entrance. With our new status, we ate at the Captain's table and Captain Nickerson began to notice that I was deeply engrossed in his ship. He even deigned to speak to me once in awhile. I spent many hours at my special spot on the afterdeck watching the Alaska I already loved slip into the fogs of autumn. It was a rather sad parting, but the anticipation of knowing I would return next summer made it all acceptable.

For a short period of time, perhaps two weeks, we moved into the up-scale downtown apartment my Dad had occupied for years. I was impressed by the fact that a doorman was constantly in attendance, and we were on a first name basis in a day or two. My parents had decided to take an extensive trip to the East and there was the problem of doing something with a thirteen year old kid. To solve the problem, I was gently, but firmly dropped into a slot at Hill Military Academy in Portland, Oregon. A part of the decision to place me there stemmed from the fact that Richard Buschmann, Eigel's third son and Frederick's closest brother, was in his last year of attendance there. It was reasoned that he would look after me. He did.

Dick was five years older than I and a sensitive and caring high school senior, a rare commodity indeed. We became very close, and I idolized him as one might idolize an older brother. We spent fine hours talking about Alaska and we spent some hours in pain speaking of the tragic accident that had killed his brother Fred. For months after the sinking, Dick had nightmares believing Fred was somewhere in the wet forests of Prince of Wales Island foraging for food and awaiting a rescue that would never come. This was only a dream. The area had been searched and re-searched. Nothing was ever found except for the skiff which had washed ashore. Loaded as she had been, the *Eidsvold* had gone down like a stone.

The student body at Hill's reflected a cross section of youth from the more affluent of the depression society. The tuition wasn't monumental, about $900 a year, but enough to preclude ninety-nine percent of American youth from attending. Within those hallowed halls, all the kids came from money; some came from more money than others. They had many reasons to be there. There were those who would dedicate to a military career and were at military school to learn how to lead men and shoot a gun. There were those who had been forsaken by parents with something better to do. Some came to learn, and some were there because they were incorrigible and inadmissible to any decent public school. It was a silver plated melting pot and I loved it.

In the course of the school year I skipped a grade, learned how to shoot better than most people, caught on to slow dancing, and spent a great deal of time dreaming about Alaska. In my spare time I built a model of the *Doris E* and one of the *North Sea*. That winter I carried on a regular correspondence with Fred Foster, now my close friend. In spite of absence and removal, my ties to Alaska were growing stronger. Dick Buschmann had a car and we drove home to Seattle for holidays. There were some times of home sickness, but my grandmother and I maintained a close and constant correspondence. That contact was always important to me.

Some good things started to happen. Men were beginning to go back to work and soup kitchen lines were getting shorter. There was a hint of coming change. Looking back, even as a kid, I could sense an awakening or an energizing among people. The lethargy of the depression years was fading and people were moving quicker and with more purpose. The war winds were stirring up dirt devils in Europe, and there were voices in the streets beginning to talk about that "Goddam Hitler," and "Why doesn't somebody shoot him!" 1939 was a pretty good year. I graduated with decent grades and returned to Seattle in the back seat of Mother and Dad's new Hudson Six. In three weeks we were headed back to Alaska.

This year was my true admission to the realities of cannery tenders and the jobs they did. I was still learning, but I knew my way about the boat and got on well with the men who worked it. The summer microcosm in which we lived had but one goal, and that was to get as many fish in cans in as short a time as possible. Fishing periods were stringently regulated by the federal government, and millions of dollars were spent before one can of salmon emerged from the line. Investors and entrepreneurs became nervous in situations like this. There was always a frenetic pace to be maintained; it was part of the "game" as my Dad said, and we all became players.

Fish traps provided by far the lion's share of the Alaska salmon catch. Ingeniously designed, these traps were diabolically effective at catching fish. The first commercial traps were constructed on patterns of driven piles from which "wire," or chicken wire was hung forming compartments which trapped or imprisoned the fish. From the trap itself, a long chicken wire fence or "lead" ran from the trap to the shore, a distance of perhaps five hundred yards. Salmon following the shoreline, would encounter the lead and turn outward paralleling the wire-netting wall. This lead led into the apex of a huge triangle from which other netting was hung. The fish were diverted into wire netting enclosures and eventually led into a "spiller" from which they could be lifted onto the collecting boat or barge by means of a dip net.

Pile traps prevailed in the beginning. That is, the trap frame was constructed of driven piling upon which the nets were hung. In many places, the water was too deep for these structures, consequently, pile traps were replaced by floating traps of the same pattern, but requiring no piling in their construction. In floating traps, nets were suspended from huge floating logs. Trap locations and operating periods were strictly regulated by the federal government which also regulated all other aspects of the industry. Without government intervention, I believe those who profited from the salmon resource would have had little interest in responsibly reducing the catch. It's easy to criticize knowing what we know now. This was the age of the adventuring investor who put up the cash and used all means possible, including theft, to widen the profit margin. In those days, conservation was a word in the dictionary, not a responsibility or a precept of life.

As previously mentioned, floating traps were similar in shape and function to the pile trap, but "floaters" were constructed of huge logs cabled together to form the patterns required to trap the migrating salmon. The chicken wire wall running to shore from floating traps was hung from a cable which was firmly anchored at the shoreline, and which was kept afloat by short logs or timbers stapled to the cable every few feet. Pile traps and "floaters" fished in an almost identical manner. Floating traps were about one hundred feet square with two large wings, called jiggers, angling out toward the shore from the side closest to the shoreline. The interior of the trap contained numerous floating logs forming the various compartments from which wire or web was hung vertically to trap the fish.

To survive even moderate weather, all logs were securely lashed together with heavy steel cables forming a huge floating "cat's cradle" or raft of enormous weight and size. Governmental regulations mandated that these traps be placed and remain precisely positioned on the site for which the permit had been approved. Deviations in positioning could mean a revocation and loss of the trap permit, thus massive anchors were employed to hold the large floating complex exactly in place.

The construction and placement of these complex forms, in a land of staggering tidal variations, was a monumental effort involving precise timing and the precise control of immense stresses, masses, and movements. There was an incredible amount of skill required to engineer success and, like a fine team of horses, it was in this arena that the cannery tender and the gigantic rigging scow came into their own. The rigging or gear scow was a huge barge absolutely essential to the construction, placement, and maintenance of a floating salmon trap. The after half of the barge was covered with a two story structure containing quarters for the crew of about fif-

This aerial fish trap view shows the essential components of the device. Web or chicken wire is suspended from the logs and the floating lead which runs to shore. The chicken wire and web forms walls which contain the fish. The fish encounter the lead in the upper portion of the photograph and turn outward from shore, passing through the angled "jiggers" and thence into the "heart" opposite the trap shack. From the heart they progress into the "pot," the central log square in the front of the photograph. From the pot they progress into the "spillers," the square areas at either end of the headlog. From the spillers, the fish are brailed into the cannery tender. The trap shack at right was the primitive home of the trap watchmen for several months.

teen men and a large galley. The forward half mounted a giant steam donkey engine and massive "A" frame. It was an entirely effective and logical contraption.

The steam donkey could skid logs across tidal flats and pull them into place for trap frame construction. The same donkey, in conjunction with the "A" frame, served as a lifting device for eight-ton trap anchors or other lifting chores as required. The working deck was large, about 35 feet wide by fifty feet long, and the whole scow could be moved by a cannery tender to any location while still providing self-contained living quarters for the operating crew. After building new traps, or repairing those used the previous year, the gear scow was towed by a cannery tender to the precise location where the trap was to be anchored for fishing. Another tender towed the fish trap to the same location. Then, with

consummate skill, the huge anchors were lowered and the trap was set in place for a season's fishing.

Following the precise placement of the trap, the same gear scow crew hung the chicken wire from the frame and the fish trap was ready for the "web crew," and the "wannigan." The web crew was responsible for hanging the cotton web portions of the trap, and the wannigan was a bunkhouse on a large scow in which the web crew was housed and fed. As in the case of the gear or rigging scow, the wannigan was towed to each floating trap where the spillers were hung by the web crew.

But, the real drama of the fish trap begins on the beach when the trap frames are built. It was a scene that merits remembrance. Dawn is breaking and the sea has just vacated an immense tidal flat, leaving behind a residue of kelp and small living things. Huge logs are lying at various angles on the drying beach, and the assault begins. The players are dressed in heavy "tin pants and jackets," a brownish canvas type of outer wear that is as heavy and unyielding as any suit of clothes can be. They are the only type of garments which can withstand the rigors of this job. The donkey engine on the scow has been fired for hours and now stands ready, breathing a column of white smoke that drifts towards the giant green forests which surround the scene. The gear scow lies high and dry at the tide line ready to align and position the jackstraw logs in a logical and pre-determined pattern that will become a floating salmon trap.

Jens Kvalvik, gear scow foreman, is the choreographer. He shouts orders to his men in a voice that transcends the loud hissing of the donkey engine. He speaks in a language half English and half Norwegian and can be heard for a quarter of a mile across the beach. Directed by shouts, his men move quickly out across the flats, some to attach chokers to logs so they can be pulled into position, while others man huge hand-saws preparing other log ends for joining. At his direction, the donkey springs into action bellowing smoke and dragging this log and that across the beach. Cables as tight as violin strings wind on drums which smoke from the tension as the logs slowly come together.

Now, cables are looped around log ends and pulled taut with the donkey engine, while men clamber on top of the huge trunks driving in staples that are bigger than their hands. Then, on to the next log which must be positioned and fastened in its precise spot, and at its particular angle. The rain begins and mixes with early morning fog turning the whole world misty and gray. Men vanish in the haze directed to their task by the booming voice of the leader. The whole of the scene is punctuated by the rapid beat of the donkey piston as it turns the cable drums, tightening the cables and stretching them to their limit.

I watch from the afterdeck with a wet mooring line in hand as the *Doris* stands off the beach breathing easily and waiting for any direction which Kvalvik might give. An errant head log, huge and unwieldy, has floated free in the night; towards noon we go across the channel take it alongside and return it to the fold, tying it loosely to a standing dolphin. We watch the action from afar since the gentle slope of the beach promises shallow water, and we cannot chance a bent propeller. There is a break for lunch, initiated by a single blast of the steam whistle on the donkey engine, then it is back to the beach and the dance begins again.

More logs, more cable, more sweat and more strain, but now there is promise for the rigging crew. The tide, in sympathy, begins to flow around the scene, erasing the beach pebbles with ripples of the incoming flood. It comes in fast and soon the entire stage is awash. The donkey engine stops in mid-haul and the whistle blows. Jens Kvalvik, cheated out of a longer working day by the fates of time and tide screams from the gear scow, "Stop boys, it's no use now, the tide's against us!" The weary men climb aboard the scow seeking rest, and sink in exhaustion to sit on anything in sight. Soon the scow and the logs are afloat in the just born flood. Jens stares at the scene, thinking ahead and forging a new offensive for the next day's tide.

The *Doris* moves the scow to a new position and she is made fast to await the next low water. One trap frame is complete and on tomorrow's high tide we will take it in tow to Pleasant Island. A 10x12 cabin is solidly anchored in the center of the trap frame. It will house two men for two months. The presence of these trap watchmen will assure that some passing fishing boat does not avail itself of a fish bonanza by emptying the trap in the middle of a dark night. Trap sites are remote, and the watchman's authority is backed up by a 30/30 Winchester should he choose to use it. The rifle is standard equipment on every trap. Some work will be done on the beach in the evening tide, adjustments and refinements to the Pleasant Island frame, but for now the dance is over and warm coffee is a welcome shield against a rising wind and driving rain.

First dawn brings a cold light to the mountain tops. For an hour a plume of diesel smoke from the *Doris* has risen, without bending, into the windless air of morning. On deck, coffee steam rises from cups held close to unshaven faces. The heavy white mugs provide some little warmth to a day beginning too early. On an order barked by Norman Hodgson, a slip line is loosed from a dolphin, and the *Doris* is backed into place against the head log of the Pleasant Island trap frame. A "Y" shaped bridle of steel cable is made fast to the trap's head log by the gear

The *Doris E* and *Service* work in tandem towing a trap frame and the gear scow to the location where the trap will be anchored and prepared to fish. Following the anchoring of the trap and the connection of the lead which ran from the trap to the shore, a crew was transported to the trap to hang the web and wire. This web crew was housed in a floating bunk house called a "wannigan," which was towed, like the gear scow, from trap site to trap site. The wannigan was fully equipped with a galley and toilet facilities... a floating hotel, primitive but comfortable.

scow crew, and the boat moves slowly ahead as the heavy tow line snakes out through an iron fairlead on the stern. Standing at the open wheelhouse door, Hodgson watches the tow line pay out. At one hundred yards he momentarily vanishes into the wheelhouse, manhandles the clutch lever to neutral, and returns to the bridge to bark an order. Phil Hastin and Bud Iverson make the line fast to the tow bit. Already, the trap is afloat in the slack water of high tide and the mooring lines are freed. In the next moments, the romance of a tow boat is born.

With an explosion of compressed air, the clutch position changes from neutral to ahead: idling injectors leap into life and send a blast of black diesel smoke high into the morning air. A sudden shudder of action and vitality runs through the boat as if a sleeping dragon had awakened. At the fantail, a welter of white and green water leaps upward and spreads across the surface as the six-foot propeller picks up speed and the vessel "hunkers down" for a better pull. In a moment of truth, the massive stern digs lower into the roiled water as the tow line leaps clear of the surface flinging off sea water rainbows in the direction of the morning sun. For perhaps a minute, there is a standoff. Hundreds of tons of floating trap logs pit their inertia against the power and will of the boat.

Then inexorably there is the beginning of movement, imperceptible at first, inches only then a foot or two. A wrinkle spreads from the stem iron at the bow then grows into a slender, rippling, "V" which frightens a gull and sends it to flight. Smoke from the stack bends backward and a tiny bow wave creases the surface. The cadence of the diesel engine builds to a constant crescendo. That sound will remain unchanged for the many hours we will be under way. In its constancy through the hours ahead, the sound will become unnoticed by those aboard. Deadened by the daily diet of engine clatter, the subconscious senses of the crew have already accepted the noise as little more than silence. The journey has begun.

It is pleasant to look back across the years and reconstruct a lifestyle that offered so much in the way of pleasure and adventure. The closely regimented and somewhat sedentary passage of hours of heavy towing, such as the situation just described, provides a canvas against which life aboard a cannery tender can be painted. I'm told, if one is to assume the role of a cultural anthropologist, the first task is to define and delimit the population he or she intends to research. Then, the investigator must examine, in turn, the communication lines, mores, physical attributes, lifestyles, ceremonies, and tools of the group he or she has elected to study. The behavior and interpersonal relationships which develop when disparate men are placed aboard a small vessel for a prolonged period of time seem worthy of such a study. Surprisingly, it seems easier to paint the picture in retrospect than when I was intimately involved.

As stated before, the thirties were a period of intense deprivation. The amenities of current times were totally missing in an era when men scrambled to feed families and keep body and soul together. There were no psychological crutches available to level out the potholes of daily living. Freud was a name just beginning to speckle the writings and thoughts of a generation whose reality could best be found not on an analyst's couch, but in the heart rending dust bowl photographs of Dorothea Lange. There were dust bowls of a sort everywhere. It is ludicrous to think of the current mania for analysis and counseling, bio-feedback, cross-cultural therapy, hypno-therapy and trans-personal analy-

Men like these, products of the depression era, were the backbone of the Alaska Salmon business. They came from all walks of life...many from logging camps and mining enterprises. Joe Brandmier, Cannery Foreman is in the center, back row. His diligence and inventiveness kept the cannery operating. My father depended heavily upon his mechanical expertise.

sis laid across those years filled with empty stomachs and cardboard shoe soles. In retrospect, it may be justifiable to conclude that deprivation might be the finest reality therapy available on earth when one seeks to develop the will and strength to survive.

Cannery tender crews were assembled almost by chance. Men sought employment, were hired and, in the beginning, placed in positions which needed filling. If chance put one aboard a cannery tender, it was pretty much the luck of the draw. In subsequent years, if an individual had functioned well in a crew, he visited the Seattle office, hat in hand, in January or February. He was probably told to "check back in April" for the same job. It was about that simple. Friendships and associations were formed among men who worked on the same tenders year after year. If they were good at what they did, they expected to be rehired and usually they were, often leaving other jobs to "go north for the summer." An experienced deckhand or engineer was an entity which enabled the boat to function more effectively. The better the crew, the better the boat. My dad never forced a crew member on any of his skippers, knowing that if he did so, he would weaken the fabric of the vessel in question. I was only a kid, working and learning, but had I not respected the rules aboard or fitted in with the members of the crew on the *Doris*, he would have removed me in an instant. I had no doubt of this.

Working on a cannery tender was a "good job" and much sought after. For those who were married, it meant a separation of six months or so; in some instances, that was a blessing for one or another of the parties involved if not for both. More important, since there was nothing upon which to spend money, a job in Alaska presented the opportunity to save wages against another depression winter. Checks were sent directly home or held by the company for dispersal in the fall. The food was excellent, the pay and living conditions were good, the work was healthy and physical, and associations with others were almost universally fulfilling. Although it might have been expected, I saw very few instances where animosity grew between crew members, and there was never an incident where physical violence developed. This is not too surprising when one realizes that under the prescribed conditions, individuals simply had to get along with one another if they were to retain their jobs and their positions in the crew. The level of cohesion among individual boat crews was remarkable considering the fact that members came from tremendously disparate backgrounds.

The cadre of crew members formed by those returning to the same boat year after year was almost always augmented with new comers who had to forge new friendships and learn the manifold responsibilities inherent in working on a tow boat. Returnees were the "dominants," and the skipper and first mate were the ruling bodies of every craft. It fell to the "new hires" and the young to adjust to the life style required to function on the crew of a cannery tender. The adjustment of newly-formed cannery tender crews was eased by the fact that those chosen to serve on a particular boat were usually hired to work on that boat for a week or two in Seattle before departing for the North. It was a good policy.

First days aboard were usually filled with great voids of conversational silence and "circling maneuvers," soft and easy treading about to determine the level and type of interaction that was required to peacefully co-exist with other individuals on board. Each crew member faced this responsibility in a different fashion, and the process of building cohesion in such a group was extremely complex. This testing and discovery phase of friendship lasted for a few days. It was usually fraught with some concern, particularly on the part of new hires. The situation was natural enough, directly akin to the reserve and hesitation exhibited when a new monkey is placed in a cage. Joking and humor between semi-strangers would begin with some small favored word or gesture which indicated the beginning of acceptance or belonging. From those beginnings, associations grew exponentially and, in the space of days, pretense could be dropped and native personalities could emerge in comfort and security.

The crew members on the tenders upon which I worked formed a true contrast. There were those, usually older, for whom their cannery tender jobs were "dead ends" in their lives and probably the best positions they would ever hold. In contrast, there were those whose summer jobs were merely rungs on a ladder leading inevitably to prosperity and a professional future. Some came from wealth and position, and some from Skid Road in Seattle's south end. Some were old and others were young. Many had already reached the zenith of their lives, and some who handled decklines and cleaned fish holds would pursue careers as physicians and surgeons, writers of renown, and entrepreneurs destined to make millions. A few were religious and many more were profane and atheistic. There were those with great physical strength and those who accomplished heavier tasks through the sheer force of will. Perhaps salient, was the fact that each boat was a microcosm of the society of the times, varied, independent, diligent, and amazingly unified.

I do not glorify these individuals through a kind hindsight. Rather, I describe them exactly as I recall them: sometimes dirty, usually smelly, often profane, steeped in a work ethic, and without exception, memorable. Most of the men with whom I worked had been hardened on the anvil of the depression. They were inured to hard labor, thankful for a job, glad to be eating regularly and most, young or old, looked for better and more promising tomorrows. My admiration of these men and the philosophy and work ethic of the times is no indictment of the present. I am not an iconoclast who would have the world turn back to the "good old days" of bread lines and infantile paralysis. I do, however, believe that adversity is a "fine and painful teacher," and I also believe that people who walk through a crucible of need are sometimes the richer for the experience when they emerge on the other side.

There was always an interesting interplay between those who worked to support a family and those who worked to seek money for higher education. Many of the young cannery tender hands were students at the University of Washington. They were invariably targeted by older hands as helpless pseudo-intellectuals, who had little ability to handle the tasks immediately at hand. Actually they were usually as hard working and effective as anyone aboard. Denigration of the young and ambitious was the only weapon of those who, for some reason or other, had missed their chance. Days were filled with ill disguised jabs at "college boys" and it was of the usual diet to hear such phrases as, *"Pardon me Professor Johnson, but if you're not studying, would you kindly hand me that goddam towing shackle?"*

Nor was this split between the college-bound and the professional sailor something new. In 1834, Richard Henry Dana, suffering from impaired vision, left Harvard University and signed on the Bark *Pilgrim* as a common seaman. In the following years he achieved immortality when he wrote of his experiences in his literary masterpiece *"Two Years Before The Mast."* Speaking with an old cook aboard the *Pilgrim*, Dana had made light of the aged man's belief in superstition, and was thoroughly rebuffed by the following statement uttered by the ancient cook:

"You think that becuz you been to college you know better dan anybody. You know better dan dem as has seen it with their own eyes. You wait till you been to sea as long as I have, and den you'll know!

This dialogue, written a hundred and fifty years ago, was a litany out of the daily conversations held on the Port Althorp cannery tenders. Nothing ever really changes.

There was a fascination to the language of a tow boat crew. The disparate methods of expression brought aboard by strangers in springtime were exposed and fried in the crucible of summer. Communication grew picturesque and became very specialized in the confines of the boat's tiny habitat. Speech, phrasing, and content were emergent and unique, created without intent by the small tribe contained aboard. Words and phrases were cooked down to a "nitty-gritty" and became a common property, commonly used and universally understood by those who shared life in a small space and had lots of time to think of new, profound, or funny things to say. There was a richness in this "tribal" language which transcended the conversational techniques and content developed by a larger population in a larger place. Not strangely, the jargon was a genetic outgrowth of two areas of social and vocational concern: boats and sex, or more correctly, sex and boats.

Words became specialized, and a sort of verbal shorthand grew by the passing days. Another boat was usually referred to as a "slab," the mast was a "stick," and the engine

Port Althorp outhouse. Places like this were a veritable treasure trove of learning for an interested teenager. Much of the information written, scratched or carved on these walls enlightened the author's growing years.

a "four banger." There was no such thing as a coffee break, it was always referred to as "mug up." Doughnuts were "sinkers," and butter was "shmear," from the Norwegian I believe. Condensed milk was "cannedcow," uttered as one word. The dignified nautical word "stern" was sometimes denigrated to "ass end," while the bow was "upfront," another corruption. Crab lice, not entirely rare on board, were known as "crotch crickets," and a rope was always referred to as a "line." Fish netting was called "web," and the propeller was a "wheel." The word "sack" always substituted for bed or bunk, and a "sackrat" was a crew member who slept a great deal of the time. There were other terms of such blatant content that it is well to ignore them and spare embarrassment.

As a fifteen year old, I was surely aware of the basic tenets of sex. In fact, I quietly considered myself to be somewhat of an intellectual expert on the subject. In actual practice, I was totally unschooled and without any practical experience. That would come some years later. My lack of experience, however, did not prove to be a detriment to the expansion of my sexual knowledge and enlightenment. The *Doris* was a classroom without equal. I'm sure my mother was aware that my education was being expanded by leaps and bounds, but probably fearing the worst, she never spoke of it. I had been dropped into a deep pool of language expansion, albeit far removed from drawing room patter. Imagine being able to learn how to cuss not only in English, but in Norwegian as well, with a little Austrian thrown in! The possibilities were limitless and I was an apt student.

There were poems and limericks and songs beyond number that became a part of my linguistic and musical "bank." I recall a short poem written on the wall of the toilet on the fish float. It went as follows:

It's no damn use
To stand on the seat,
The crabs on the Sally
Can jump ten feet!

The poem referred to a possible infestation of lice on the *Sally S,* our sister boat, and was almost surely scratched on the wall by a member of the crew of the *Doris.* I recall passing the *Sally* close aboard one day while we were outbound to a trap location. As we passed, Bud Iversen shouted across to the crew of the *Sally:* *"I'd rather count towels in a whorehouse than crew on the Sally S."* It was a wonderful retort, filled with imagination and meaning. I never forgot it. The *Sally's* crew responded with multi-lingual curses and gestures that are surely universal, but Bud and his well turned phrase were the champions of that encounter. The confrontation made our day. Plain old fashioned cussing and sexual overtones colored most of the language used by the crew. There was really no iconoclastic or erotic intent involved; it simply became a way of communicating and, after awhile, the speaker became anaesthetized to its content and effect. I had the good sense to recognize the fact that what was proper for the crew was not proper for a fifteen year old kid. If I had even thought about using the boat language which constantly swirled around me, the skipper or Phil Hastin would have done me in. Just hearing the stuff was in itself a right-of-passage; I was not expected to use it. That didn't stop the learning process and I tucked away all the crew's words and phrases in the back of my mind so they would be with me when I grew a little older

There were many rituals among the small and exclusive groups which constituted the cannery tender crews. One universal was the "mug up," or formal coffee break which occurred mid-morning and mid-afternoon aboard every tender I ever knew. This group meeting was convened in the galley, and the ever present coffee was accompanied by doughnuts, bear claws, muffins, or whatever else the cook had prepared. Attendance was an obligation unless one was on watch in the wheelhouse or engine room. Many tenders had small doors cut in bulkheads or overheads so that coffee might be passed through to the individual on watch, such was the necessity for at least a semblance of inclusion. These meetings were part social and part business and, if the galley served as the tribal altar, the coffee mug was the tribal icon.

I hold now a duplicate of the coffee cups used aboard every tender I knew. I believe it to be the most utilitarian vessel ever conceived. This one bears an embossed eagle and the initials USA on the bottom. It's about a quarter of an inch thick and every bit as heavy as it appears. The handle is massive and loops poetically down from the rolled lip of the cup forming a sort-of half heart shape. The cup is almost imperceptibly flared from bottom to top and the bottom edge is comfortably rolled to preclude any rough edges. These cups are glazed a seemingly indestructible glossy white which shows every nuance of coffee stain. This is not a problem however, since stains can be licked clean or erased in a second with a wet thumb or forefinger. A little research has disclosed the fact that these cups were originally used on navy ships and thus are usually referred to as "Navy Cups," no matter the manufacturer's name. Whatever their history, they were a part of life on a cannery tender and as utilitarian a device as the wheel or lever.

Navy cups were practically indestructible. They could be dropped on a section of steel, diamond-plate decking without cracking, breaking, or denting the deck. They were strong enough to pound nails, and I don't remember ever seeing one which had been chipped. However, the most important blessing of this holy grail was its amazing capability to retain heat. Picture an early dawn on a deck partially awash with a vicious swell, add a stiff wind and pelting rain bringing genuine misery. These cups held not only coffee, but a tiny, blessed spot of warmth that suffused the hands and faces of men who were really cold. It's nice to think that they were also filled with a measure of confidence and hope. Perhaps around the next point it might warm up a bit and the rain might stop for a little while. The combination of strong boiled coffee and the warmth of a Navy mug were enough to make one realize that a driving rain and freezing wind couldn't last forever. The coffee we drank was usually a primitive, boiled coffee made in a huge blue-flecked enameled pot on the back of a *Shipmate* stove. Ground coffee, water, and a raw egg were brought to a boil and, after a prescribed time, a dash of cold water made the grounds disappear like magic to the bottom of the pot. The coffee was delicious and a fitting libation to accompany the ceremony of "Mug Up."

Fred Foster rang a small hand bell to announce mug up time. The crew of seven

filed into the galley in an order which would allow each member to slide conveniently into his particular and inviolate spot. On the *Doris*, the Skipper sat on the port side of the long athwartships table then, in order, sat the Mate, the Chief Engineer, his assistant, and the deckhand. I was relegated to a spot on the table's starboard end, on the outside, so I could be sent on errands of minor importance if necessary. Foster poured the coffee and each consumer added "cannedcow" and/or sugar to his particular taste. There was a ritualistic stirring period following the pouring of the rich, black liquid. This stirring was a precursor to conversation which was almost always initiated by the Skipper. Sugar users drank their coffee with the spoon in the cup, held in place by a crooked thumb. This was a macho device which allowed the individual to periodically stir the brew and thus assert his personality. Stirring was also a defense mechanism used to gain time to create an effective retort in the verbal sparring which always constituted an important part of the ritual. I thought it something akin to a gunfighter whirling the cylinder of a revolver before a shoot out on a dusty street; on the tender the missiles were words, not bullets.

Fred Foster's freshly made dough nuts or other pastries were passed out to the participants in order of importance. The skipper was always served first. It was as if he were a designated taster for the group, the only one capable of assessing the true value of the goodies proffered by an overworked chef. Like a wine taster, Captain Hodgson sampled, then nodded his agreement that the fare could be shared by his child-like underlings. An anxious Fred Foster constantly hovered over the table, dishtowel in hand, waiting for the inevitable praise that was so much a part of this tribal ceremony. The galley was a mini-cathedral in a savage land, always warm and inviting. It was an edifice conducive to ceremonies and ritualistic proceedings, a nice place to be. I, for one, always left it with reluctance to join again the wet decks, wind, and rain outside. I suspect it was that way with everyone.

Usually the skipper began the audible phase of the mug-up in a low, barely audible monotone, questioning the mate about the boat. "Was the towline chaffing? Was the compass course certain to clear Althorp Rock? How about that port side fender that had been torn on a trap log?" For some minutes the dialogue was a shared thing between Hodgson and Hastin. The galley remained silent save for the bell-like clink of spoons stirring coffee which had already been stirred enough. Then Hodgson would spear his next target, and the continuing liturgy might go like this: "Claude, that goddam forward winch is leaking oil on the goddam deck. See if you can't fix the goddam thing today before somebody steps in the goddam mess and goes overboard." Claude, who had already filled the top half of the galley with blue smoke from his Sherlock Holmes pipe replied, "I gotta get a new seal for that thing Norm...we'll have to order it from Ketchikan when we get back to the cannery." After a swallow of coffee, Hodgson would reply, "OK but don't forget to order the goddam thing. Every time I look out the goddam wheelhouse window I see that goddam oily patch and it's driving me nuts!"

Then, in all likelihood, it would be my turn. "Hey Eddie, did you clean out that goddam paint locker like I told you yesterday?" Not waiting for an answer he'd continue, "I swear if you was my kid I'd drown'd yah...too goddam lazy to do what you're told and too goddam dumb to learn how to play crib...you better get me about five of your old man's cigars when we get back or I'll kick your ass right off this boat." When I interjected that I had cleaned out the paint locker, Hodgson lowered his head slightly and mumbled something like "oh" into his coffee cup. Kato Schwalling, Second Engineer, tried to suppress a giggle and was impaled by Hodgson's dark eyed stare. "What's so goddam funny Schwalling...want your ass kicked off this tub too?" Kato stirred a little more vigorously biding for time and said, "Skipper, this slab'd sink without me and you know it." Hodgson's "Hrrmmp" reply was directed into the bottom of his tilted coffee cup.

And so it continued, a board meeting without portfolio. We were emissaries from every corner of the land meeting our regent in a ceremony designed to keep the *Doris E* alive and well. Before the board meeting was adjourned, each ambassador would have his coffee and his say. These small conclaves permitted the skipper to assess the welfare of his tribal constituents. No matter how much coffee was left in one's cup, when the Skipper rose to leave everyone else did too. Fred Foster, still clutching the ever-present dish towel, dispensed his aura of Sloan's Liniment everywhere he went. Mixed with the acrid smoke from Claude's pipe and the remnant vapors from Bud's roll-yer-own Bull Durham cigarette, the galley smelled a little like a cross between a hospital and a stock yard. That was probably the reason Foster left the doors open.

On board the *Doris*, card games were a constant. If one were not on watch or in the sack, he was likely to be found near the coffee pot or in a card game at the galley table. Other than solitaire, two card games were dominant among the crew, Cribbage and Pinochle. The latter, without exception was always pronounced "Piss-knuckle." To call it anything else would have been an ethical violation. Even the count in cribbage was made somewhat picturesque by the addition of shipboard "enhancements." If one were playing crib, at the end of a hand he might count aloud, "Fifteen two, fifteen four, fifteen six, and two is eight and a fart's a fraction!" It was a cliché that was used so often that's only its absence would elicit attention.

During towing journeys, which sometimes lasted several days, games were played around the clock with hands being passed from one crew member to another as the watches changed. Since long hours of participation honed the skills of everyone involved, the quality of the play was close to professional. Over weeks and months of constant engagement between crew members, small nuances of difference in playing techniques were detected and exploited. Nobody cheated and I remember no money ever being involved. The games were a part of the rite of belonging and, as such, cemented and solidified the connections between those involved. Naturally a skill-hierarchy of players developed with each crew member trying to ascend the pecking order and those on top of the "food chain" snapping at those below. Every game was played in true, cut-throat fashion with no holds barred.

The card ritual, regardless of the game played, was always a table slamming, oath-filled, raucous procedure, and the attendant noise carried even to the engine room where it could sometimes be heard over the sound of the laboring diesel. Counts in cribbage were recorded on an old non-descript board with broken bits of wooden matches used as pegs. I felt there was a need for change. For several weeks I labored secretly on a new cribbage board for Norm Hodgson and the *Doris*. I carved it from a piece of yellow cedar I'd found in the carpenter shop. The wood even smelled like Alaska. There was a relief of a whale, a mountain, and some salmon on the top and I made special pegs for it. In spite of all the work involved, I remember being a little embarrassed about giving it to him. At that age I didn't realize the gift was a dead giveaway indicating the great affection I felt for the man. I brought it to him one forenoon when he was in the wheel house by himself. For a few moments there was some surprise, then he put his arm around me as any man should do to a kid. He turned away, and I was amazed to think he might be having a little trouble with tears, so I left. I never expected anything like that. It was an unforgettably nice thing that happened to us both. The crib board was always used after that and had a special nail in the galley upon which it was hung. Like the hanging pots and pans, I recall after awhile, it wore it's own little marks on the wall from swinging back and forth with the roll of the *Doris E.*

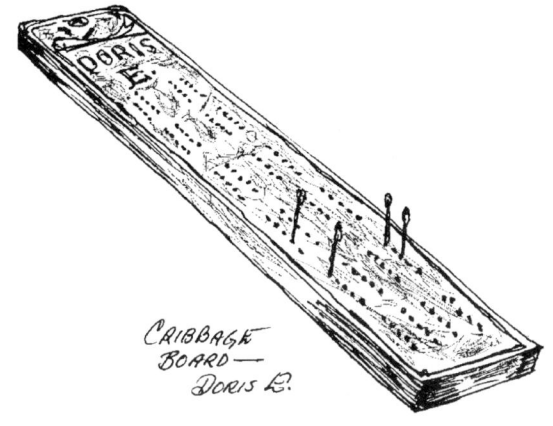
CRIBBAGE BOARD — *Doris E.*

Wheel watches on cannery tenders were "subject to change without notice" dependent upon the tasks in which the boat was involved and the area in which we were working. As a kid, I never stood a night wheel watch unless it was for a short duration in open waters. Such responsibilities were for those older and more experienced than I. But, on those rare occasions when I did find myself alone at night on the bridge of a tow boat, my heart expanded and I found an excitement and thrill never before equaled in my lifetime of fifteen years. It was the fulfillment of a dream. Seventy-two years of living have failed to dull my love of those times of solitude and night-beauty or my capability to relive them again in memory.

Wheel watches were divided among the skipper, the mate, and the deckhand. They were assigned on the basis of time and the difficulties which might be encountered during various portions of the passage. The skipper was always on the wheel in hazardous waters and the mate in those places not considered extremely critical. The deckhand and I were assigned day and night watches in open waters only. The wheel watch change involved an interesting interplay between crew members. It was an informal and emergent ceremony of sorts, a naturally occurring phenomenon, and I recall no one ever had to explain to me or to anyone else the protocol surrounding it. If one's watch were to begin at four in the morning, he was expected to arrive in the wheelhouse a few minutes early or at the very least, on time. The wheel was never forced on the new watch. It would have been unthinkable for the individual who was being relieved to relinquish the wheel and immediately depart. It was traditional to grant some courtesy time to the crew member taking over. I never saw this tradition overlooked. Wheel watch changes were like a changing of the guard. A position of trust and ultimate responsibility for the boat and the crew was passed from one individual to another. With that responsibility, the gift of patience to the new watch was inviolate.

Night time watch changes were the most dramatic. Getting ready for a two or four hour night wheel watch involved a toilet session of one kind or another, or perhaps both. Then followed a face washing, even a tooth brushing if one were just emerging from the sack. There were deck shoes, sweaters and jackets to be put on, and probably a cigarette to be lit. Hair was sort of brushed about by hand and a wool watch cap pulled on to cover the disarray. The journey to the wheelhouse was interrupted by a trip to the dimly lit, quiet and empty galley for a cup of hot coffee, a spoon with which to stir it, and one of yesterday's doughnuts, which could always be found under a dish towel on the galley table. As one walked or staggered to the wheelhouse dependent on the sea, the doughnut was always clenched between the teeth leaving an inboard hand free for emergencies. There were no railings amidships and the danger of falling overboard was always present.

Cannery tender doorknobs were another universal, identical on every boat I ever saw. They were cast of massive solid brass, perhaps the size and shape of a goose egg, and polished by the turning of years of coarse and callused hands. They protruded from large, heavy brass latch boxes which were always, in contrast, greened by weather. In a world of utilitarian machinery, I never considered these doorknobs as being totally functional. When wet or cold, they were hard to turn, and wheelhouse doors were always sticky and hard to open. It was usually necessary to set the coffee cup on the wet deck, keep the doughnut in clenched teeth, and use both hands to open a sticking wheelhouse door. Such an entrance was so often required that it seemed a part of the ceremony.

Once inside, the crewman coming on watch would gaze slowly about for a minute or two then gravitate toward the red binnacle light above the compass, stare briefly, and mutter some sage statement like,

"It's as black as Coalie's ass out there, where in the hell are we?" The answer might be, *"We're about seven miles south of The Sisters Islands; that's the light blinkin' over to the right. We've got to stay out quite a ways from the lee shore, the goddam trap keeps dragging us off to port, and there's a rock off the next point. There must be a hell of a current running, I think we're bucking the tide...we're not making doodly-squat as far as speed's concerned."*

By this time the new watch had turned toward a chart pinned to a table at the rear of the wheelhouse. Picking up a flashlight which was always left in the same exact spot, he would turn it on, covering the lens with his fingers thus allowing only a tiny portion of light to escape. White light was an enemy which would temporarily blind all on the bridge. For perhaps several minutes, there would be an examination of the course and the surrounding obstacles then the flashlight would go out and welcome darkness would again provide ambient light for the helmsman. There would follow some few minutes of jokes or carping about this or that while the watch replacement took sips from the still hot white mug, then a new hand on the wheel and the statement, *"OK, I got it"* would signify the changing of the watch. A relieved crewman never left at once. There were always lingering minutes and words which built an inclined plane allowing the new helmsman to slide easier into the hours of aloneness that lay ahead.

It took a little over two days to tow the Pleasant Island trap frame to the anchoring location. Another two days were required to anchor it in place. The *Service* had towed the huge gear scow bearing the mooring anchors to the site and, in concert, the process was begun. The *Doris* and the *Service* were like sheep dogs worrying the trap frame and gear scow into position for anchoring. Everywhere the action was intense. Men and equipment worked in a frenzy. Black diesel smoke from the two tenders blasted into the air as the boats bullied the scow and trap frame fighting against the inertia and heavy tides racing through the straits. Like a captured locomotive, the donkey engine on the scow bellowed steam and noise as cables strained to raise and move the eight ton anchors required to hold the trap in place. Shouted orders from Kvalvik, the scow foremen, rent the air and shouts and curses rang out across the roiled water. Men carrying long pike poles, dressed in heavy tin pants, jackets and hobnailed boots ran full speed across the tops of the slippery trap logs pushing here, pulling there, belaying or casting off cables and lines. The scene was replete with noise, smoke, action, tension, and danger. The whole of it washed with an everlasting down-pouring of rain and the constant, raucous cry of displaced gulls. The scene is ever-fresh to me. There was much of a drama there.

When the monumental task was completed, men and boats seemed drained of strength. The Pleasant Island frame was now firmly anchored in place. Looking like some giant array of jackstraws, it flexed its flat, monstrous log body as it rode the heavy swells rolling in from the open Pacific to the West. A few days later, the web crews would hang the netting which would turn the trap frame into a fishing bonanza, a wooden money-making machine. During the ensuing weeks, a river of salmon would swing east from the open sea past Cape Spencer. In an unbroken stream of millions they would traverse Cross Sound and head further eastward through Icy Strait, searching for the streams of their birth. On the north shore of the Strait, the Pleasant Island trap awaited the coming flood. Swimming in profusion, the fish would encounter the long chicken-wire "lead" hanging vertically in the water like a fence and running from the trap to the shore. Confused, they would turn outward and enter the open and waiting mouth of the trap complex from which there was no escape. Ten floating fish traps provided the bulk of the catch for the cannery at Port Althorp. Each one had to be positioned and anchored in the same back-breaking manner. The closer the trap location to the open sea, the more hazardous and difficult the installation became. It was a task of major proportions.

Our work at Pleasant Island was finished and, while the *Service* towed the gear scow to the next trap location, we would return to the cannery and tow another trap frame to a meeting with the *Service*. The logistics seemed simple on the surface, but the vagaries of monstrous tides and unpredictable weather made trap installations a virtual high-stakes crap-shoot. In many instances, trap frames were pounded to pieces before a single fish was caught. The cost to build, equip, and set a floating fish trap in place was about ten thousand "1939 dollars." The amount, at that time, was a fortune and the gamble was enormous.

Without a tow, it was a run of only a few hours back to the cannery. We left late in the afternoon and, in two hours, we were abeam Lemesurier Island running easily in a moderate sea and bucking a slight wind and current rolling in from Cape Spencer. I was in the galley talking with Fred Foster when the seemingly everlasting cadence of the engine broke into a disastrous clatter. I jumped out on deck and saw puffs of black smoke leaping from the stack. In moments, the hiss of compressed air signaled the clutch control had been moved to neutral and the engine shut down. A silence as pervasive as any noise imaginable filled the evening. As the propeller stopped rotation, the *Doris* slowed in mid-channel and soon lay dead in the water wallowing drunkenly in the moderate swell.

Claude and Kato Schwalling, who had raced to the engine room at the first indication of trouble, were joined in minutes by the rest of the crew. After a brief examination and consultation, the trouble had become painfully clear. She had been run too far and too hard. Early that season, there had been a scorching, full-speed run to Juneau with an injured gear scow crewman. That emergency voyage and the pressure of our long tow had severely scored a cylinder wall. Nothing could be done on the spot. For some time, we drifted eastward with the tide. It was a new and hurtful learning experience. For twelve years the engine had performed flawlessly, often running for days with scarcely a shut down. The Washington Estep diesel and the *Doris* herself had been new and "breaking in" when Lindbergh took off in 1927 on his epic flight to Paris. The strong heartbeat had continued unceasingly through years of other momentous events until these now silent moments off the south east end of Lemesurier Island. After some discussion between Claude and the Skipper, the fuel supply to the offending cylinder was cut off, and the engine was cautiously restarted. We limped slowly past

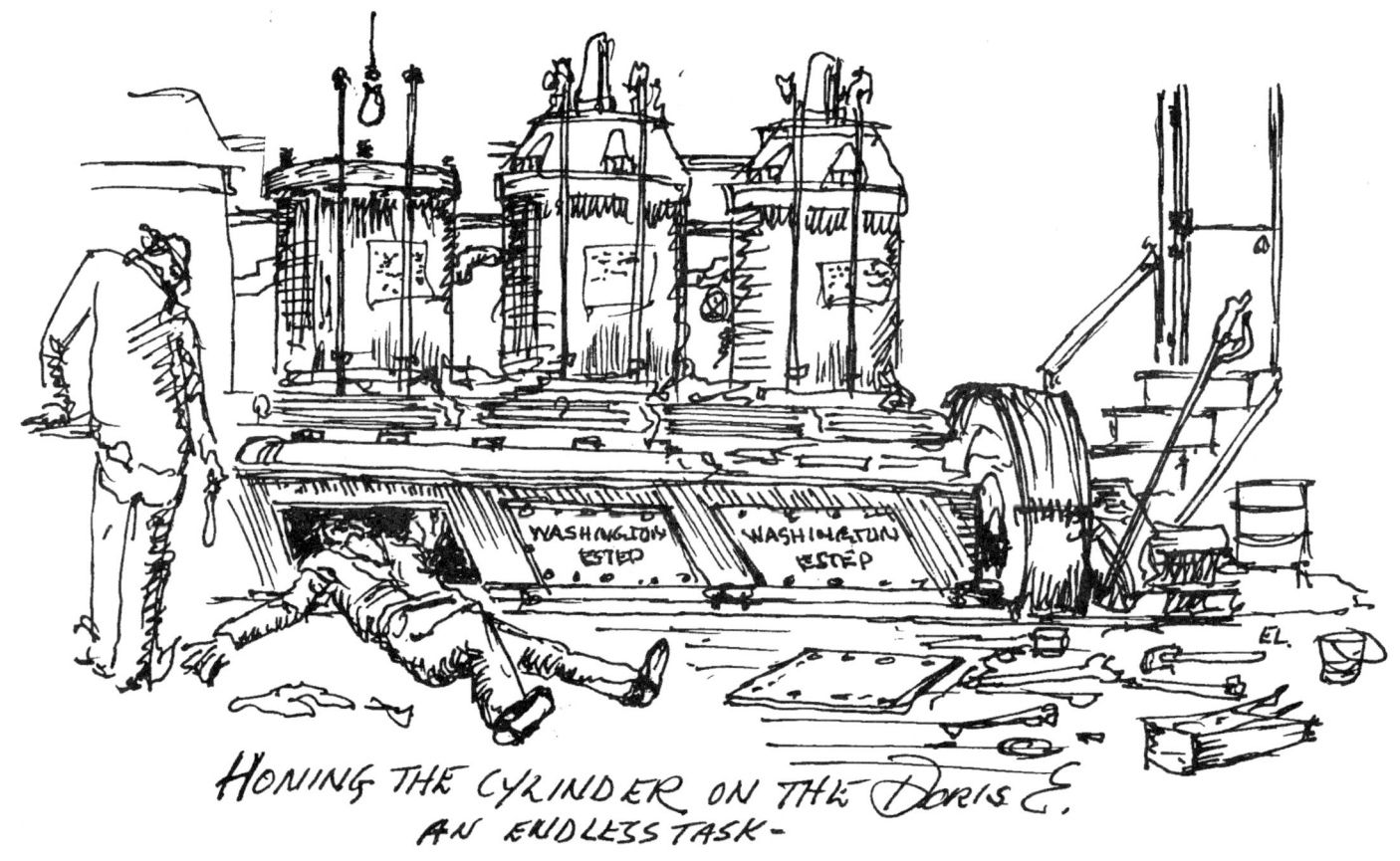

HONING THE CYLINDER ON THE *Doris E.*
AN ENDLESS TASK -

Althorp Rock and back to the cannery. Young and impressionable, I viewed the breakdown as a mortal body-blow against boat and crew, but there were those aboard who saw it as a respite from the trap towing regimen which lay ahead. Regardless of each crewman's perspective, one thing was certain; everyone aboard became suddenly and painfully aware that nothing lasts forever, and nothing should be taken for granted.

The breakdown could not have occurred at a more inopportune time. We were now a boat short in the critical race to get the traps located and anchored to meet the deadline for the start of the fishing season. As soon as the *Doris* was made fast to the fish float, the effort to repair her began. Work would continue around the clock until she was up and running again. As previously mentioned, the engine was massive. To provide access to the huge cylinder head, a hatch had been cut in one of the stateroom floors over the engine room. With a portable hoist or "come-along" mounted in the stateroom, a cable could be lowered into the engine room and the cylinder head, weighing hundreds of pounds, could be carefully raised and set aside. Next, the inspection plates lining both sides at the bottom of the enormous engine were removed, exposing the crank throw and connecting rod of the number three cylinder. The strength of two men on an open-end wrench at least three feet long was required to loosen the massive cap screws holding the connecting rod to the crankshaft. The piston, with connecting rod attached, was then pushed downward in the bore. With total compassion and care, the connecting rod was carefully led out through the inspection hole followed by the massive piston. It was precisely as if the engine had given breech birth to an endangered child. The greasy obstetricians congratulated each other and the crewmen stood about contemplating the miracles of the re-generation of life. The heavy piston and connecting rod were lain carefully on cotton waste in the corner of the engine room, truly products of an immaculate conception. The only thing missing were the Three Wise Men. There was joy in the engine room.

A small electric bulb was lowered down the top of the cylinder bore to examine the extent of the damage. It was plain to see a hell of a job lay ahead. If one lay on his back, arching painfully over the engine bed plates, he could stick his head into the massive crankcase and peer upward into the open cylinder bore. Portions of the wall were as shiny and smooth as a polished mirror, but an area of the upper middle portion had been savagely scratched and marred by heat and the scraping of a damaged piston ring. There was only one way to effect the repairs. An individual had to crawl halfway into the crankcase and, with a small piece of fine emery paper reach up blindly into the bore and smooth out the gouges and ridges by endlessly rubbing the damaged wall.

It was agonizing work but there was no alternative. The fumes from the crankcase were sickening, and the exertion of reaching up into the cylinder bore was so exhausting that one could work for only a short period of time. Norm Hodgson was anxious that I not miss anything in the way of sea experiences on my way to maturity; thus, I was quickly assigned to take my turn with the rest. After a very few minutes at the task one emerged with a sore back and a head spinning from the fumes in the crankcase.

The boat crew and some cannery workers impressed for the job labored three days to erase the damage. In the engine room, a bucket brigade of workers waited their turn to rub the cylinder wall until their arms seemed about to fall off. Slowly but surely the scrapes and ridges melted back into a smoothness that one could feel and admire; the worst was over. Norman Hodgson and Claude ran their fingers over the repairs and pronounced them acceptable. On the back seat of an ancient airplane, a new piston and set of rings were flown to Port Althorp from Juneau to be installed in the engine. Like Lazarus, the *Doris* rose from the dead and rejoined the land of the living. It was a good thing. The next day, in an ongoing pattern of trial and tribulation, the *Lloyd C* smashed into the fish float crushing the fish elevator and precipitating a minor catastrophe for the cannery. It was an apt action for the bimbo, street-walking slab that she was.

Water-powered fish ladder smashed by the rampaging Lloyd C which the author's father referred to as "the scourge of the sea." Oscar Larson was not enchanted by the existence of the direct reversible marine diesel engine.

If I have spoken ill of the *Lloyd C* it is no more than she deserved. In granting life, breath, and personalities to the cannery tenders that filled my life, I have no responsibility to love them all. The *Lloyd C* was a loser and the aforementioned accident was no fault of her victimized skipper or crew. It happened because she was a recalcitrant hulk that shirked an honest day's work and spent her time stumbling around causing problems. A part of the trouble with the *Lloyd* was her engine, a Direct Reversible, Fairbanks Morse which my Dad described as, "An abomination of the Seven Seas!" Oscar Larson had experienced several incidents of "reverse failure." To fully understand his disdain, I must offer the reader a short course in primitive diesel engine mechanics.

The engines which powered these boats were antique behemoths, products of a long-gone era of engineering. There was only one reason the engines were still around; they ran forever. Since boats have no brakes, the propeller must be turned in reverse to stop a craft's forward motion and to prevent it from running into things. This reversal of the propeller is normally achieved by the use of a clutch. One of the big problems in early-day diesel engines was the size of the massive clutch equipment required to make a boat back up. These clutches were huge, power-wasting affairs, heavy and ineffective, providing perhaps only half as much power in reverse as was supplied when the boat was going ahead. To simplify things and solve these clutch problems, a diabolical genius somewhere designed the direct-reversible marine engine.

In the direct reversible engine there was no clutch. If one were going full speed ahead and wished to stop or back-up, the engine had to be brought to a complete stop then restarted by a blast of air to run in the opposite direction. The theory was brilliant, but there was one fatal flaw in the concept. If the engine happened to stop at a particular place in its rotation known as top-dead-center, it could not be started again until the massive flywheel was carefully turned over by hand. There was never time for that. One can imagine the difficulties encountered when the smiling skipper, approaching the dock with fifty tons of cannery tender and one-hundred tons of loaded scow, demanded reverse and didn't get it. The accounts are legion! Boats under docks, scows and skiffs run over, masts knocked down and people hurt. The direct reversible engine was a real-life, two-edged sword, to be avoided if possible. Such was the heart of the *Lloyd C*.

On this particular morning, the treacherous tub was approaching a landing at the fish float. There were docks on both sides, thus no escape from the inevitable. When the skipper rang down for astern, there was a deafening silence followed quickly by an ineffectual blast of compressed air, followed by a warning blast of the whistle, followed by a loud crash as the *Lloyd C* in all her glory ran into the fish dock at about seven knots! The violence was followed by a screaming string of invectives flowing from the wheelhouse window as the skipper witnessed the carnage and called on all the Hounds of Hell to "destroy the sonofabitch that made that engine!"

This encounter was moderate. It took carpenters two days to repair the float and fish elevator. It was a minor miracle that no one was hurt. On a previous occurrence, with a direct-reversible diesel some years before, my dad had seen a cannery tender go under the dock full speed, tearing off the wheelhouse and injuring several of the crew. Skippers of direct-reversible tenders learned quickly, without fail, and always approached a dock at a shallow angle. Aboard or ashore they also walked about with a constant feeling of paranoia, never knowing when they were going to run into something. As previously stated, the *Lloyd C* was a loser and we all knew it. She spent the balance of the summer looking for something else to run into; thankfully, she didn't find another target.

The canning season of '39 rolled on rather smoothly. I spent almost all my time on the *Doris E*. It was the kind of summer a kid would dream of, an idyllic half-world, midway between child and man. I admired the men about me and tendered equal respect to the college sophomore or the skid-road refugee. In turn I was taught the developmental tasks one has to know to grow up. I stood my watches on the boat with more confidence and maturity and my vocabulary, good and bad, increased by leaps and bounds. At times, in the evenings, I rowed ashore in quiet bays and carefully fished for Dolly Varden trout, always keeping an eye out for bears. Deer haunted the lonely shores and there was a constancy of life and movement everywhere. Often I fished off the stern for rock cod and halibut. The waters were teeming with fish. I'm sure some of the shores I walked had not felt footsteps in this millennium.

The author at right with 175 pound halibut he caught off the stern of the Doris with a homemade lure. Pictured above left to right. Thor Torstensen professional wrestler, Duncan Robertson, later to become a physician, Kato Schwalling, and the author. The halibut was given by the author to the crew of the Doris who traded it for liquor at Elfin Cove. The author got not a swallow.

Toward the end of July, I complained one night to my mother about a persistent itching on my knee. I had noticed a small reddish patch about the size of a quarter which was apparently the source of the trouble. For a week I treated it with Lifebuoy soap and a wash rag, probably not the most effective medical regimen. After a cursory examination, she came to the conclusion that I had fish poisoning and was about to lose my leg. My dad said that was nonsense. Mother ruminated over it for a few days, longing for some contact with the medical profession. Perhaps the breaking out was a manifestation of scurvy, the ancient mariner's curse; after all, I was working on a boat, wasn't I? Or maybe it was beri beri, or cholera, or how about a vagrant strain of malaria or some other tropical disease that had worked its way from Uganda to Port Althorp? The die was cast, Eddie was going to the doctor. I have always suspected that the trip had a two-fold purpose. I'm sure she felt some concern about my knee. I'm equally sure she needed a little respite from cannery life. For her, a chance to see a doctor, any doctor, would be a high point in her summer.

A day or so later, Alex Holden, a good friend of my dad's who was a co-founder of

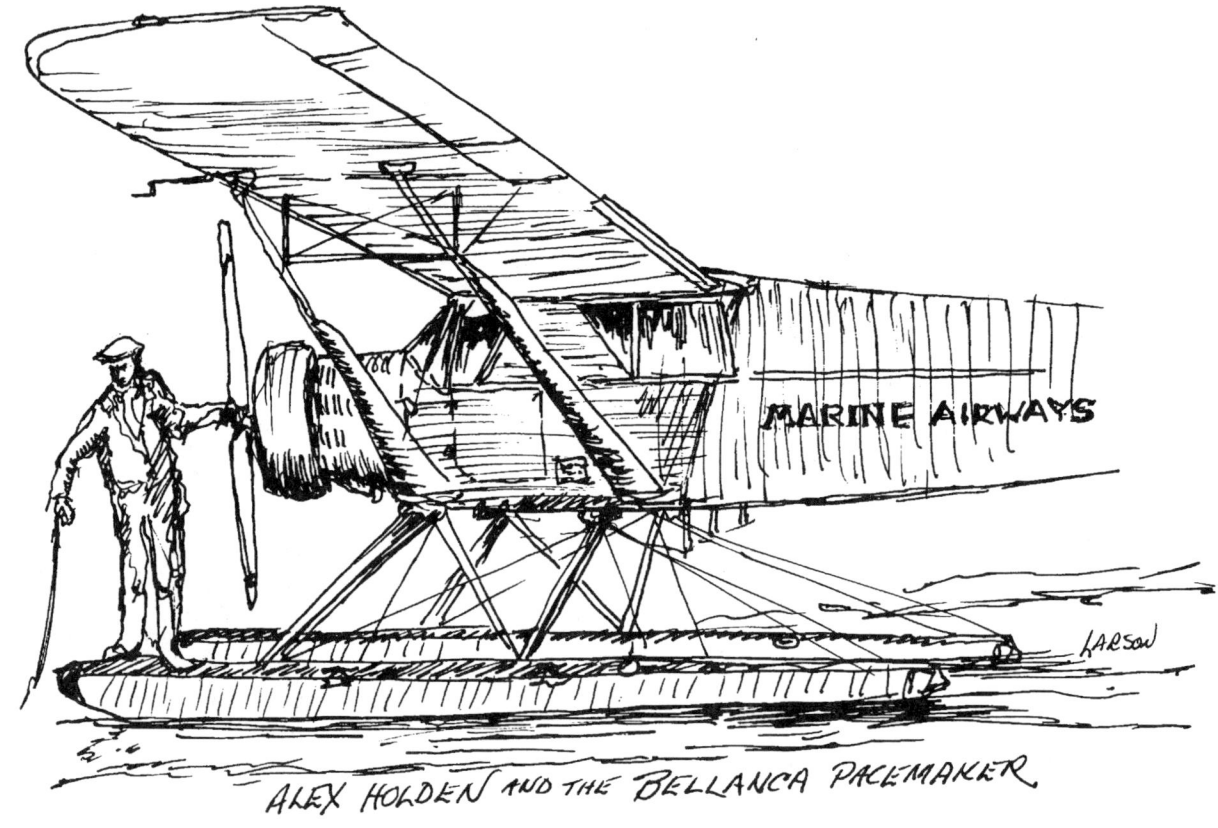

ALEX HOLDEN AND THE BELLANCA PACEMAKER

Marine Airways, flew in to Port Althorp to pick us up. Naturally I claimed the front seat in the old Bellanca Pacemaker high-wing monoplane, and in minutes I had started poking at things. The Pacemaker was like most aircraft that ended up in Alaska: plain, simple, and hard-used. The instrument panel, dented and worn, was covered with old compass courses written in pencil that were never erased. This airplane had been nick-named "Shaky Jake" because of a tendency to flap its wings in turbulent air. It was a huge slab-sided machine with immense windows. Even in 1939, she looked like a museum piece. There was some history here too. A year and a half before I climbed into the right seat of the old Bellanca, it had been warmed by a man destined to become an American legend. Alex Holden had taken a young nondescript reporter of the Washington Daily News for a free ride over Taku Glacier. The passenger's name was Ernie Pyle, later to become the most famous war correspondent of World War II. Of the flight Pyle wrote, "I have superstitions about airplane pilots. For instance, I have complete confidence in a pilot who is bald-headed, and practically none at all in one who has a mustache." Pyle must have really enjoyed Alex, he was as hairless as a cue ball.

Starting up and idling, the old Bellanca was as noisy as a threshing machine in a cane field. Holden shouted in my ear explaining the procedures for take off. As I looked in the back, I saw my mother was white-knuckling her arm rest and Dad didn't look that great either. At the speed of a fast walk, we pulled away from the landing float leaving behind four or five cannery hands who had held on to the airplane while we got on board. After about fifty feet, Holden swung her into a slight breeze from the East and shoved the throttle open. The results were anything but electrifying. With the Bellanca it took a little while for anything to happen. Finally the plane made a reluctant decision to get going. As we picked up speed Alex began moving the stick violently forward and aft. This action, of course, threw the passengers forward and backward in their seats as if they were on a hobby horse. He hollered something in my ear like, "Gotta shake her loose!" In a moment the floats got "on plane" and she broke free of the waters of the Bay, shaking off salt water like a wet Labrador.

We climbed east over the salt chuck opposite the cannery and, in five minutes, the meadows and crags of Chichagof Island were flashing past hundreds of feet below us. Here was a new sphere of adventure and joy. In ten minutes I had become hooked on flying. The flight to Juneau took about forty-five minutes and I talked with Alex Holden all the way, asking questions and taking in a new world. We flew beneath a broken cloud deck with yellow bars of sunlight breaking through highlighting the sensuous yellow- greens and acid-blues of the solid Spruce forests below us. The feeling was ethereal, almost spiritual. I would get to know it well in the years just ahead. At cruising RPM, the engine felt like velvet and the propeller spun a sun-lit disk about three feet in front of our faces. Holden must have liked kids; he pointed to the jiggling instrument panel explaining the messages each needle was sending out as he spoke of the functions of every switch and lever. There weren't that many; before we got to Juneau I knew them all by heart. He was still talking as we let down over Gastineau Channel and flashed over the docks under a lowering sky. I looked down at the pontoons and waited, then in a moment white feathers of spray flew out from the floats as we settled gently down on the water, a perfect landing.

We taxied up to the Marine Airways Terminal, which was little more than a large unpainted garage on floats fronted by a wooden ramp extending out into the water so aircraft could be pulled out for storage or repair. The walls were lined with tools and "airplane junk." At the edge of the ramp, three men were fueling a Lockheed Vega with a hand pump out of a fifty gallon drum. My dad introduced me to Shell Simmons, a partner of Holden's who, like Alex, was a legendary bush pilot. Some years before, Simmon's face had been savagely beaten up by a collision with an instrument panel in a crash off Chichagof Island. He was badly scarred. Characteristically, in the same accident he had ignored his own injuries and saved one of his passengers from drowning. As I stood by the Vega with my parents the fueling was completed. We moved a little away as they cranked the engine for starting. Apparently the mixture was too rich and gas dripped from the cowling, ran down the ramp, and turned the water into a round rainbow. When Simmons hit the starter again the whole thing took off in flames. It was fairly spectacular until the prop blew out the fire. Simmons shut down the Vega and climbed down laughing. My mother's face was blanched white in fear as she said, "My God I'm glad that didn't happen to our plane!" Simmon's chuckled and said, "Hell, Violet, they both do that all the time!" The statement added immeasurably to her "white knuckle flying syndrome."

As expected, my ailment was a ringworm that was completely innocuous and non life-threatening. After spending a couple of days in Juneau at the Baranof Hotel, we met Alex Holden at Marine Airways early on the third day for the trip back to the cannery. The return trip captivated me. An early sun had lent a wealth of color and clarity to the forests, the land and the sea; the day was simply unforgettable. Alaska flying is an experience not to be missed. It's true that the weather may be sour at times, there is also an occasional bit of peril in the mix, but in this land, the sheer wonder of the scenery and the freedom of flight come together to stagger the imagination. One crosses whale-laden bays and immense meadows holding alpine lakes that no one has ever fished. High crags reach up, covered with snow and ice that has not melted since the dawn of time. Even as a kid, not given to much sentimentality, I felt my heart expand in the immense grandeur and freedom of the morning. The spell lasted all the way from take-off to touch down. Too soon, Alex turned low over the cannery and set the Bellanca down flawlessly. We had become friends on the two flights. In the years just ahead there would be a lot of airplanes in my life.

Trap shack and watchman, a hazardous job. On rare occasions the traps broke up in heavy weather and watchmen were forced to row ashore and live off the beach until rescued by a company tender or other passing vessel.

The days slipped by as the fishing season started well. There was a good run of fish this year. My Uncle Charlie, now eighteen and seeking money for college, had gotten a job as a fish trap watchman. I saw him rather frequently when the *Doris* brailed or emptied his trap. He and another kid about his age shared watchman duties on a trap located in Icy Strait, a rambunctious stretch of water northeast of Chichagof Island. Life for the watchmen was tough, demanding, and primitive. The only shelter was the small cabin bolted to the trap frame which provided only elemental protection against the winds and rains that are a part of Alaska's birthright. With one small door and one small window, the shack was barely large enough to hold two bunks, a small storage area for provisions, and a tiny coal stove for cooking. Toilet facilities were so primitive they need not be described. About the only other amenity available was a heavy wooden skiff used to escape the trap frame should it start to disintegrate in bad weather. To appreciate the job fully, the reader must be aware that the shack was fastened insecurely to a bunch of logs that rode the rough waters, rising and falling violently twenty four hours a day. It was not an admirable life style. Watchmen however, were essential to the successful operation of a fish trap. Not only did they constantly work to keep kelp and debris out of the trap, repair web and change lines, they were also the first line of defense in discouraging "fish pirates" from robbing the trap.

Hijacking salmon from a company trap was looked upon as a "Robin Hood action" by many seine boat operators of the time.

There was a certain feeling abroad that stealing from the "rich" was OK. A definite difference of opinion existed in this area of thought. Obviously, owners of the traps considered such individuals to be the equal of horse thieves and deserving of the same treatment—hanging from a cottonwood tree. The practice of robbing traps was widespread and of genuine concern to those who had invested thousands of depression dollars in setting up a salmon trap. My dad had "no truck" with trap robbers and employed a couple of small trolling boats to patrol the traps and discourage any such nonsense. In the final analysis however, the security of the fish trap depended entirely on the honesty and diligence of the two watchmen involved, most of whom could be counted on to perform the jobs for which they were being paid. Unfortunately, there were some exceptions.

The process of fish-trap thievery was basic and took two forms. In the first mode, a boat skipper might pull up to a trap and simply suggest that the watchmen might be interested in selling some fish for cash. Surely, in some cases, this approach worked. The second scenario was different. Some skippers became rather insistent about raiding the trap and advised the watchmen that if they didn't get in the trap shack and keep their mouths and eyes shut, they might end up as fish food. I submit that the second approach was the most productive. The crime usually occurred at night, preferably at a time when visibility was minimal. The seine boat would pull up alongside the trap head log and, contingent on the method of coercion used with the watchmen, would then simply brail the trap fish into his fish hold and be gone before anyone was the wiser. It was an easy way to make a lot of money, but sometimes it didn't work out that way.

It was getting late in the season and my mother insisted that I spend a few days around the cannery helping her with some household chores such as finally cleaning up my room, doing some laundry, and catching up with obligatory correspondence. As a teenager I found such chores to be pretty loathsome, but there was no escaping the fact that she had made up her mind. As a result of her justified badgering, the *Doris* sailed off without me and I spent the ensuing couple of days doing precisely and exactly what she told me to do. Because of my dedication to housework, I missed a true Alaskan adventure, namely, the Great Fish Trap Robbery of 1939. It was a saga of good guys and bad guys, replete with a great chase scene; I never forgave my mother for making me miss the performance.

The *Doris* had been out for a couple of days on trap maintenance chores and was returning early to the cannery to pick up some scows. Dawn was just breaking through a light fog when she passed the Point Augusta trap and saw my Uncle Charles waving his hands frantically from the head log while pointing to a retreating seine boat. Drawing closer they heard Charlie shouting that the seiner had just stolen salmon from his trap. With no more ado, Norm Hodgson swung the *Doris* around in pursuit of the fading seiner and its crew. The *Doris* was no speed demon, but with some bolt washers jammed under her push rods she bellowed out black smoke, voiced some objections, and picked up additional speed, heading down the strait like a jackrabbit. Hodgson had called Juneau on the radio and advised the U.S. Marshall that he was in pursuit of a fish pirate and needed help.

With passing minutes, the distance between the *Doris* and the seine boat shrunk as the chase continued. The seiner was experiencing a bit of a speed handicap in the fact that her fish hold was half full of pink salmon that belonged to somebody else. In a futile effort to widen the gap, the men on the seiner began to lighten the load by pitching fish overboard, one at a time. It was a futile effort. The distance between the "Chaser and the Chasee" shrunk until the tender's bow was only inches from the stern of the skinny seine boat. Then, in a scene reminiscent of a Tom Mix movie, Bud Iversen threw a line over the seiner's stern cleat and snubbed it down to the *Doris*'s forward tow bit. The show was over. The two boats were lashed together and remained so until the U. S. Marshall, aboard an Alaska Fish and Game boat, arrived on the scene. He proceeded to confiscate the seiner and arrest the crew. The craft was towed to Juneau, where the seine boat skipper received a jail sentence after trial in Federal Court. I remember telling Norm Hodgson how sorry I was to have missed all the excitement. He allowed as how it would be "goddam nice to get some kind of a reward for doing something good around here," and suggested I get a couple of Dad's Mozart cigars for him and for Claude Graham who'd shoved the washers under the push rods of his engine to increase the tender's speed. That wasn't a request, it was an order with which I naturally complied.

The curtain was coming down on the salmon season of 1939, and the cold winds from Glacier Bay had already begun to blow. Some small snowfall was collecting in the dished mountain that rose behind the cannery as the geese were leaving for someplace warm. The traps were safely beached and secured at the head of the bay. Hopefully they would ride the tides of winter and remain in one piece. By this time, some thought of "denning up" for the winter had undoubtedly struck the minds of Chichagof's great Brown bears. I begged to be allowed to go south on the *Doris* but my dad put his foot down. I had a last cup of coffee and a muffin with Fred Foster, waved good-bye to the boat and the crew and watched until she was out of sight past Althorp Rock leaving only that summer of memories and a last faint smell of diesel smoke. We waited a cold and rainy week for the *North Sea* to take us back to Seattle. It was a lonely time without a cannery tender around.

Winter...
and the season of 1940.

Thor leaped into the boat jumping toward the stern and levering another shell into the rifle's chamber. The bear was only feet away from the stranded skiff when he fired again hitting the sow full in the face--still she came on.

The trip home was full of pocket books and shore watching for me. It was also a great opportunity for my mother and dad to relax over scotch and sodas, a pursuit not totally foreign to their nature. Upon arrival in Seattle, I was enrolled in the rather exclusive Lakeside School for Boys, pretty much against my will. The school was rather elitist and I had been a little too poor for a little too long to comfortably fit in with Seattle's more affluent prep-school group. It wasn't their fault, it was mine. Norman Buschmann had been in attendance at Lakeside for a couple of years and, after settling an altercation over his pouring water in my bunk we became good friends. Norman was a strange young man. Although our relationship was one we both enjoyed, there was a part of him which I could never reach and which he could never show. Some of the time he appeared isolated and walled-up inside himself. It was a seeming detachment that was confusing to me. He expressed little in the way of emotion. It was as though he swallowed both the good and bad things in his life and really didn't feel them or speak of them. I have known buffeted men like that, but Norman was only a kid.

One thing we shared was a common interest in boats and Alaska. Under the expert tutelage of his father, Eigel, Norman was a first rate tow boat skipper by the time he was fifteen. It was as if he'd been born to the task and was blessed with a fisherman's genes. Eigel Buschmann was always kind and involved with both of us. He worked hard, in his way, to strengthen the bond between Norman and me. Norman had few friends and perhaps I was the only game in town. At any rate, we got along well, bowling and boating together but really sharing little else. Eigel and his wife Nora still nursed a burdensome sadness at the loss of Frederick the year before. I recall that Norman and I never discussed his brother's death. That was a little strange.

We had no sooner returned to Seattle than Leif Buschmann, Eigel's younger brother, suddenly died of a heart attack leaving his wife Esther, a daughter Lorraine, slightly older than I, and Leif Jr., a son just my age. I saw little of Leif Jr. while we were growing up. We were cordial at family parties and got along OK, but he seemed eons older than I. At sixteen I felt he smoked too much, drank too much and drove his 36 Ford roadster too fast. He was out of my league and I guess I took a certain amount of satisfaction in that.

Grade-wise I performed at a mediocre pace at Lakeside, not really enjoying the blessings of a costly and stratified institution. I played football because I was expected to play football; I was not very good at it. I also played basketball which I loved. I was very good at that. One day after a basketball game I was introduced to the first girl who, up to that point, had ever really impressed me. She was a lovely teenager, bright, enthusiastic, verbal and charming. Her name was Kathy Brazeau and she listened and laughed when I talked to her. We attended a couple of dances together and she came to see me play in a couple of Lakeside basketball games. She was a friend and the kind of a girl one always remembers. Our relationship was simply a couple of kids laughing and having fun together. In that era of innocence, it was all right to have that kind of relationship. I think those times were better because of that. After I left Lakeside I never saw Kathy again although her fate would be inexorably linked to Alaska and the salmon business as was mine.

Time turned the corner into 1940 in a world that was steeped in war. Britain and France were hanging on by their toenails as Hitler's Germany was taking over everything in sight at the point of a gun. Worse than that, millions of German lemmings were holding up their hands in a stilted salute to their paperhanger leader while the elite of their society were building ovens of hate and prejudice that would mark them barbaric for generations to come. An unrest and concern for coming conflict crept across the nation replacing the hardship and deprivation of the depression. It became evident that we would soon be involved. April saw the invasion of Norway by the Germans. That had a personal ring to it. The invasion deeply touched many of the Norwegians I knew who were involved in Alaska fishing. There was a strong cohesion among these people. They possessed a profound dedication to an ancestral home and nation that many of them had never seen. I also saw in them a primitive and burning determination to restore freedom to that homeland. The feeling prevalent in the Norwegian community made it clear the German invaders were not to be envied.

Port Althorp in spring surrounded by awesome, snow-covered peaks. The tenders await chores. From the left: the *Hero, Service, Doris E* and *Sally S.*

In January of 1940 I insisted on attending a public high school. I registered at Seattle's Roosevelt High, finding it much more suited to my needs. I bought my first car, a 1928 Chevrolet from my uncle, for the princely sum of one dollar, and began to peer at girls with amazing frequency. During the winter months I recall going with my dad to the shipyard where the tenders were moored off season. They were all there, The *Doris, Sally, Service, Hero, Eagle* and, as he would say, "the goddam *Lloyd C.*" I particularly recall one gray day he was there on business. I borrowed a key from the Port Captain and wandered through the *Doris* as she sat wintering in the cluttered waters of Lake Union. There was a wetness and cold about her that was hard to reconcile with the warm, active and alive creature I so admired in summertime. Fred Foster's galley was damp, and still. There were no doughnuts on the table. Norm Hodgson had taken the cribbage board off the wall; there was not a pack of cards in sight. I remember going up to the wheelhouse and having trouble opening a door that had stuck shut from months of moisture and non-use. Inside, the wheel was frigid to the touch, the windows were streaked with dirt and the old foghorn I'd spent so much time polishing was green with tarnish. There was something that seemed "dying" about her and I didn't stay too long. What I had thought would be a good idea had turned into a portent of something ahead that made me uncomfortable. I recall not feeling very good about things when I took back the key.

I have read somewhere that 1940 was not a good year for California Cabernet Sauvignon. It was not a very good year for the Larson family either. In late-May I came home from school one day complaining of a bellyache. I went to bed, but things got worse. That night I was carted off to the hospital for an emergency appendectomy. I missed a week or so of school and had to work like hell to catch up. I was still a little "off my feed" when we boarded the *North Sea* for the trip to Port Althorp. I had hoped to ride north on the *Doris* but because of the operation my mother wouldn't allow it. The trip north was now a familiar experience including the usual bumpy crossing of Dixon Entrance. At that point it didn't bother me anymore. When we got to the cannery everything sort of fell into place and we began preparing for the coming season. I took up part time residency on the *Doris* and the world was back in its orbit.

Activity at the head of the bay was as frantic as ever. The gear scow worked each tide preparing traps to be towed and anchored, and the tender fleet labored through endless hours fulfilling their tow boat obligations. The peace and beauty that surrounded this place was rumpled by the drama of noise, motion, confusion and action that made the head of the bay a tidal war-zone. The gear scow crew was unique and well fitted to match the violence of trap preparation. Many had been previously employed as loggers or in other heavy-duty occupations. With them, refinement was not even a minor concern. They were employed to do jobs that required the utmost in strength; intellectual capacity was as little a part of their job as a pair of spats and a necktie. Among this crew was one of the favorite men of my life, Thor Thorstenson. His first name was pronounced "TOR," and sounded as if one were addressing a Neanderthal or Cro-Magnon man.

Thor had worked for my dad for many seasons, laboring on the gear scow through the summer months, then taking his money and fading into the labyrinth of Seattle's lower end in the winter. He was one-part flower and one-part gorilla, possessing a mixture of gentleness and power which set him apart from the toughs that constituted the gear scow crew. He spoke with a heavy Norwegian accent and carried himself with the grace of a natural born athlete. Thor was well over six feet tall and weighed between 230 and 250 pounds the bulk of which was concentrated in a massive pair of shoulders which were difficult to get through doorways. During the winter, Thor augmented his summer wages in a fascinating fashion; he was a professional wrestler. Appearing as the Masked Marvel, dressed and masked in crimson attire, he terrorized Seattle's winter wrestling circuit and picked up the few bucks required to maintain his primitive life style. I really liked this man as did everybody else.

One evening Thor decided to do a little trout fishing. Putting together a fly rod, he rowed to the shore from the gear scow anchored a quarter mile away. He had tucked a 30-30 trap rifle in the skiff just in case of emergency as he looked forward to a pleasant evening of quiet fly fishing. The small creek that emptied into the head of the bay was running bank full and amber-colored with June snow melt. Thor beached the skiff on a gravel bar close to the mouth. Taking his rifle and fly rod he worked his way up the margins of the creek wading through berry vines and tide grass always damp with summer rains.

Through all the years, I have recalled this spot as a semi-circular arena of sheer beauty. The bay here was usually mirror-still. A tawny tidal meadow ran from the shoreline for two hundred yards inland, ending in a solid stand of spruce which signaled the forest's beginning. Behind the trees, the carpeted mountains climbed to granite crags filled with snow. Eagles and Ospreys criss-crossed the mountain faces vying for fish, or somebody else's carrion, and there was a brightness of wild flowers seasoned by a soft evening wind which made the place quite simply, spectacular.

Thor had fished for about an hour moving slowly up the stream from hole to hole, and had jammed about fifteen good-sized Dolly Varden trout on the dried spruce branch he used for a creel. The faint wind had shifted to the north, blowing from the tree line. He first saw the female Brownie as she pushed through the underbrush perhaps seventy-five yards away. Being upwind she got no smell of him and lumbered slowly through the grass swinging a mammoth head from side to side as she moved toward his fishing spot. The rifle lay about twenty yards away on the bank. Thor crouched and started running toward it and toward the skiff which lay grounded on the gravel bar a hundred yards beyond. It may have been his movement or a crushed twig that alerted her. She rose up for a second, looked, spotted the running figure, then charged through the tide grass and willows after the Masked Marvel.

Thor grabbed at the rifle as he ran past, levered a shell into the chamber and swung toward the charging bear in desperation. He fired one shot which caught the animal twenty-five yards away full in the throat and knocked her down. Levering in another shell he fired again hitting her foreleg. She roared and rolled about in rage as he turned running for the beached skiff. In seconds she was up again and racing after him.

He reached the skiff with the bear only yards behind him, and pushed desperately at the bow trying to launch it. The tide had dropped slightly and the heavy rowboat only pivoted on the gravel, inches from the receding tide. Thor leaped into the boat jumping toward the stern and levering another shell into the rifle's chamber. The bear was only feet away from the stranded skiff when he fired again hitting the sow full in the face—still she came on. The firing had attracted the attention of the men on the scow and they crowded the railing and watched powerless as Thor, with huge leaps, rushed into the water with the crazed bear only feet behind him. Hip-deep in the freezing water, Thor turned and fired again at point-blank range. The bear reared up screaming in a welter of foam, blood and kelp throwing water everywhere then dying in the amber shallows five feet from the beach.

With the whole gear scow crew looking on, Thor trudged wearily from the water and sat resting for a time on the gunwale of the skiff. Then, laying aside the empty rifle, he dragged the bear's carcass above the tide line and into the grass. A couple of weeks later as the crew looked on from the scow, Thor went again to the beach and worked over the rotting bear carcass for some time. He returned with the animals teeth and claws which that autumn were made into a necklace by a Seattle jeweler. Phil Hastin told me that the Masked Marvel never appeared at Seattle's Civic Auditorium again without his bear tooth necklace which was carefully removed from his massive neck before the match actually began.

Trap preparation went well that year. Although the rain was drenching and incessant, the moon sun and earth lined up and huge spring tides made the work easier for Kvalvik and his crew. Work, like the rain, was ceaseless, and the engine on the *Doris* throbbed the days away, never ticking into coolness, never shutting down. Essential oil changes were made on the run so to speak. When the last bolt was tightened, a blast of air brought the engine back to its life of labor. As soon as all the trap frames were ready, the task of towing them to their locations and anchoring them in place began. The five tenders bullied their charges about night and day while the gear scow was constantly

On a more relaxed fishing expedition, Thor seems to still be looking for bear. From the left, Thor, Bo Swapp, the author and Phil Hastin. Phil was the best of fishermen and usually directed such expeditions.

on the move from one location to the next. Everyone was wet and worn; the constant draperies of rain and fog became an ongoing depressive reality. Boat crews and the gear scow crew worked in a condition of perpetual wetness, half salt water, half rain. It was down your neck and up your sleeves. Shoes became moldy and clothes could never be fully dried out. Comfort was a commodity that seemed to have vanished from everyone's daily existence. My mother felt the strain of weather and loneliness and demanded that I spend some time with her and with my dad at the cannery. In her enforced idleness, she began to count the days it rained. She stopped at fifty-four realizing it was only an exercise in futility. It was easy to curse the land and its cruelty at times like that.

I had been at the cannery for several days while the *Doris* was towing traps. None of the tenders were in port, and periodically I spent time on the dock looking wistfully to the north, waiting for something to show on the horizon, much akin to a dog waiting for a bone. I was on an evening errand when I first saw the *Sally* rounding Althorp Rock pouring out a string of black diesel smoke that spelled trouble. She would not have laid down that kind of smudge were she not running faster than she was supposed to. I watched her approaching with no let up, until she was fast to the fish float. Nils Sagsted, her skipper, climbed the ramp and brushed by me saying, "Don't go down there Ed." He meant exactly what he said and I watched him half trot toward Dad's office. In a minute, and without a word, both men strode past me at a brisk walk headed for the tender. From the dock I could look down on the *Sally*. Finally I noticed the blanket covered object on the after deck. Sagsted and dad talked for several minutes, then my dad bent down and pulled back the blanket that covered the body of Leonard Huven of the gear scow crew.

Leonard was a tough young kid, well suited for trap work. He was a strong and an able worker. Because of a sense of humor that was constantly in force, he was well liked by the crews on the boats and the scow. He was about twenty years old, flax-haired, Norwegian, and always friendly. This was his first—and last—season in Alaska. As with most boat crews, there was always an air of horseplay among the members of the gear scow crew. After being assimilated into the group, it was natural for one to try to express some individuality and thus impress those about you. The scow, working at the Three Hill Trap, had shut down at noon to wait for a tide change. Talk began quite innocently about the giant A-frame on the scow. In the course of conversation the question arose; Did anybody aboard have guts enough to dive from the top of it?

The A-frame was the dominant feature of the huge gear scow. Constructed of huge timbers for lifting the trap anchors it soared about fifty feet above the water. The joking continued as Leonard left the group returning minutes later in a pair of trunks and nothing else. Kvalvik was napping in his quarters and none of the others aboard chose to stop Leonard as he began climbing up the wooden ladder. Whether he "chickened out" or made the dive it would be fuel for mug up for the rest of the season. The crew said there was no hesitation when he reached the top. He shouted down something like, "Okay you bastards, watch this!" He arched his body out, fell, and hit the water with his head tilted backward. In moments he rose back to the surface as if in a seizure. One man jumped from the bow and dragged him close enough for the others to reach down and pull him from the water. By the time he was stretched out on the deck, the tremors and his breathing stopped. Leonard was dead.

The top of the "A" frame of the gear scow was perhaps fifty feet above the water level, a dangerous and demanding dive. The water was brutally cold.

The next day Alex Holden flew in with the Bellanca and Leonard's body was flown to Juneau for return to Seattle. A feeling of sadness permeated the cannery and everyone connected with the operation. It was a senseless and needless death, the loss of a young man's life without rationale or reason. The everlasting rain continued to fall.

Weather was and continues to be a vital ingredient in the mix of Alaska salmon fishing. Always a factor, sunshine and flat seas were a blessing while storms were ruinous. Midway through the 1940 season, a violent offshore storm sent its resultant swell and waves racing around the North end of Chichagof Island raising proper hell with those traps closest to Cross Sound and the open sea. One of the trap frames was disconnected from its lead and rapidly torn apart by the huge western swells. The two trap watchmen were lucky to escape with their lives. With no way to communicate the peril which faced them, they were somehow able to launch the trap skiff and row ashore where they spent a miserable two days, wet, cold, hungry, and without shelter.

A cannery tender routinely sent to check their condition and that of the trap picked them off the beach two days later. They were returned immediately to the cannery for recuperation.

If the trap frame broke up in heavy weather, watchmen rowed to the beach and waited for rescue by cannery tenders or passing vessels. In many instances when bad weather persisted, they were stranded for several days with minimum food and shelter. My Uncle, Charles Rehm, rowed ashore in a damaged skiff after a trap break up. He spent one night ashore with a small fire and sought shelter in the lee of a small pile of boulders. Sick and cold he called it, "the longest night of his life."

I have previously mentioned that there were two basic types of cannery tenders in general use, those which carried fish in their holds and those which were in fact tow boats, and had no fish hold. Tow boats brailed the catch from the trap into a scow positioned between the boat and the trap during the brailing process. In heavy weather, only those tenders which had a fish hold could brail traps located closest to the open ocean. Brailing into a scow in rough seas was out of the question.

All cannery tenders were equipped with massive "fenders" which protected their hulls during towing or brailing operations. These huge fenders were throwbacks to sailing days. They were works of art made by an old cannery hand who had served under sail and still practiced his knotting and braiding skills. The fenders were, in fact, like huge sausages with cores of old manila hawser tightly wrapped, then encircled by a closely woven covering of heavy manila line. The finished product, which weighed hundreds of pounds, bore a large loop on either end. Finished, they were twelve to eighteen inches in diameter, about six feet long and virtually indestructible.

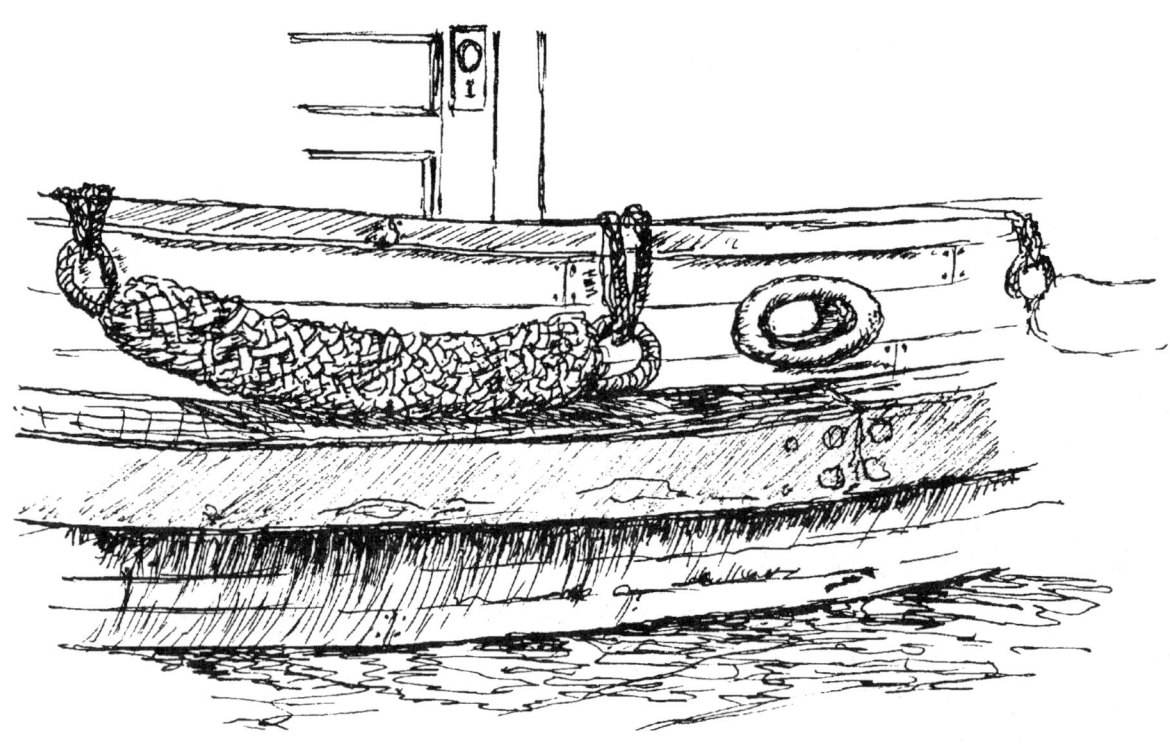

The forward loop of these fenders was made fast to a huge iron ring inboard of the toe rail and the aft loop was equipped with a heavy line by which the fender could be lowered or raised over the tender's rub rail to protect the hull. They constituted a first line of defense. Without them, a cannery tender simply could not survive.

It required awesome skill to handle a tender during trap brailing in heavy weather. In retrospect it seems the men chosen to skipper these craft were possessed of some sixth "sea-sense" that allowed them to operate boats in weather which everyone else might shun.

They assimilated the vagaries of tide, swell, wind drift, and weather, threw in the variables of their boat's power and capability, and each day took their small craft to the edge of peril. Almost invariably they made it through. Never were such skills more required than when approaching and brailing a floating fish trap on a really rotten day. From two hundred yards away, the skipper had to close on the massive trap head log at just the correct angle, account for tides, wind, and drift, then time his approach to avoid larger swells which might raise the tender high then dash it against the trap face. Once the tender was made fast against the head log, there was still a dangerous and constant "working" between the boat and trap frame, both of which rose and fell at different rates on the passing swells. The aforementioned manila fenders and their ability to absorb punishment was the only thing that made a mooring against the trap face possible.

On those traps closest to the ocean, fenders were useful but not enough. The head logs on "outside" traps were equipped with massive wooden stanchions, twelve to fifteen inches square, heavily braced, rising eight or ten feet vertically above the head log. When brailing outside traps, tenders moored for protection against these stanchions. Their purpose was to preclude the possibility of a massive wave picking up the tender and smashing it down against the top of the head log thus crushing its hull. On many occasions, the stanchions served their purpose. When heavy seas were running it was not unusual to see, from the deck of the tender, the entire trap frame incredibly inclined against the face of a blue-gray swell that was totally frightening in its immensity. It was as if the frame had been laid down against the slope of a moving blue mountain. The sight was unforgettable.

Once the brailing or emptying process began, the net had to be lowered again and again into the spillers of the trap. Each time, thousands of wriggling salmon were dumped aboard the boat, some going into the hold and others flying everywhere imaginable. The

deck was soon covered with flapping fish and a layer of slime which made the footing slippery and hazardous. Every time the brailing net with a load of fish was raised toward the boom it dumped an ample load of cold sea water, fish scales, stinging jelly fish, kelp, and other marine horrors on the deck crew. Passing swells brought boat and trap frame into constant loud and jarring collisions, upsetting the footing, and setting the top rigging and brailing net into a dangerous swinging pattern. If one adds to the picture the added dimensions of a cold wind, sea spray, and driving rain, the portrait of trap brailing becomes nearly complete.

Deck winches of the time were primitive contraptions, reminiscent of the wheel and lever stage of man's development. They were equipped with a hand operated friction band which provided lifting power while a simple foot pedal control, when depressed, applied the brake. The heavy gear above our heads was totally controlled by this ancient device which was usually rusty, worn, and smelled like fish. The safety of the deck crew hung on the chief engineer's ability to properly work the brake pedal with the bottom of his slimy rubber boot, not always an easy task. In really bad weather everything above deck including the cast iron pipe on the brailing net, mast shrouds, and running gear was set into a vicious lateral motion by the passing swells and the constant banging of the boat against the head log. It should come as no surprise that the deck crew cast many looks aloft to be sure the whole rig was not coming down on their collective heads. Brailing an outside fish trap was a daunting and dangerous task.

Among the more repugnant tasks rotated among the tenders was that of towing out the gurry scow. In the canning process there is a constant outflow of fish entrails that must be disposed of. The extent of this problem can be understood when one realizes that in times of heavy fishing, the cannery operated 24 hours a day. This round-the-clock activity produced an incredible mass of fish heads, tails, and entrails. From the canning machines this "gurry" poured down a wooden chute into a huge box known as the gurry scow. The scow was perhaps thirty feet long by twelve feet wide and ten feet deep with barn like doors on either end. The forward doors opened toward the rear as did those at the aft end of the scow. When both sets of doors were opened, and the scow was towed through the water by a tender, the tons of entrails were flushed out by reason of the scow's forward motion. There was only one problem, someone had to ride the scow to deep water and, at the skipper's direction, open both sets of doors, closing them again after the rotten task was finished. Fish gurry had to be dumped in deep water in the center of the bay. If disposal were made in shallow water such as that close to the dock, the fish heads would rot on the bottom, fill with noxious gas, then rise to the surface like a balloon, giving off an odor that was overpowering. In some instances, the resultant stench created a chemical reaction so strong it blackened the white paint on adjacent buildings.

Unlike a fine wine, fish gurry does not improve with age. After a week or two, the collection of offal produced a stench that set the head to spinning. Such was the prevailing condition on the morning the *Doris* was directed by my dad to make the tow. I, in turn, was selected to ride the scow. I have little doubt those arrangements may have been the result of a plan devised by my dad and Norm Hodgson; no matter, the die was cast. Access to the gurry scow was accomplished by climbing down a ladder at the face of the dock. The ladder was immediately adjacent to the discharge chute from the canning machines which, unfortunately, were in full speed operation at that particular time. A constant flow of fish entrails poured in to the already full scow, splashing about and covering my oilskins with scales and various and sundry body parts of fish, some old, some new. The *Doris*

backed into the face of the dock and the tow line was extended to me on the end of a pike pole. No one wanted to get too close. The crew aboard seemed to be enjoying the situation to the utmost, experiencing a great deal of laughter and making caustic remarks.

I attached the line to a forward towing bit on the scow, and the entourage pulled slowly away from beneath the chute which continued its awful outpouring into the waters of the bay. At this point, the scow was so loaded, the top was almost awash. I was left standing on a timber, perhaps a foot and a half wide, with water swirling around my rubber boots as the *Doris* pulled us slowly toward the middle of the bay. The run to the dump site required about twenty minutes. Our arrival at the spot was signaled by a shout from Norm Hodgson on the bridge that I should open the front and rear doors of the scow allowing the gurry to be flushed out. We had very little headway as the forward rods were raised and the front doors came slightly ajar. I then turned toward the scow's aft end to open the rear doors. I had taken several steps when I slipped on the narrow walkway and fell head first into the loaded scow.

It was later related that this singular accident had happened to others. Some had even been fortunate enough to fall outside the scow. For me, it was an incomparable experience. There was, of course, the specter of drowning, but even worse was the disgusting fact that I had plunged, head first, into a box containing ten feet of rotting fish remains.

When I surfaced, a slimy line was close at hand which, with a foot hold, allowed me to pull myself out of the disgusting morass. The effort was a miraculous combination of strength and motivation; the cold water was not even noticed. When I was free and sitting on the walk way with my legs in the gurry, I wiped my eyes and saw that what had probably been some consternation on the tender had turned into hilarious laughter. Another mini-legend had been created at my expense.

Fearing to try walking again, I slid back and opened the rear doors. The *Doris*, amidst gales of laughter and shouts, picked up speed. In two hundred yards, the gurry scow was at last purged of the remains of a couple of weeks of canning. When the scow was clean and the doors closed and fastened, the towline was taken in and I climbed aboard the tender leaving a trail of indescribable droppings behind me. I was soaking wet and covered with gurry, an unacceptable entity to be aboard Norman Hodgson's boat. He ordered me to sit and drip on a section of coiled towline until we got back to the dock. "Goddam kid, yah could'a drown'd back there screwin' around like that, next goddam time we have to dump that goddam scow you can try it again and see if you can get it right." In an hour, news of the incident was all over the cannery. Repeated shampoos and tub baths helped, but for the next few days, my mother was the only one who got very close to me, probably in the belief that I might need a doctor. I'm sure she felt another couple of days in Juneau at the Baranof Hotel might help to round-out the summer.

During the course of the 1940 season, I became increasingly close to Fred Foster. That summer he celebrated his 84th birthday with a cake of his own making. The strength and endurance of this ancient man was a continual source of amazement to the crew and to everyone who knew him. Cooking on a small towboat during a busy Alaskan fishing season was a Herculean task. Few were able to sustain themselves on the constant regimen of work in small quarters compounded with limited facilities. In a time and place experiencing a constant turn-over of cooks, Fred was unassailable and forever. The cook's day began long before daylight, included a short rest period in the afternoon, then a full surge of powering up for dinner preparation and doing dishes. I doubt he could have endured the strain at his age had he not built a wall, behind which he could periodically retreat; Fred Foster was an inveterate and insatiable poet.

Fred's stateroom, complete with the ambiance of Sloan's liniment, was immediately aft of the galley on the port side of the *Doris*. It was an effort for Fred to raise his aged and bent frame from the deck to the high step half way up to his cabin door sill. I wondered then about the knee pain he constantly suffered and endured. He possessed a special kind of courage. On a small table just inside his cabin door stood the ancient Underwood typewriter upon which he composed his primitive poetry.

On evenings after dinner when the galley was empty and clean, save for the ever-present coffee percolator, the sound of Fred's hunt and peck typing system issued from his half opened and curtained stateroom window. The clicks were sporadic as the creative process waxed and waned. Now a line, then another, then silence. The efforts were reminiscent of a weary woodpecker. Fred was reaching for words and the sound was an integral and inseparable part of my memories of approaching nightfall aboard the *Doris*.

In the off-season, Fred lived in a small houseboat moored in the Duwamish waterway in the west end of Seattle. I knew where he lived, but never visited his place because we were never invited there. I'm sure it was humble at best. Periodically, he sent poems to me through the mail. They were on different subjects: honesty, character, fidelity, happiness, things like that. I read them all, and for awhile, I saved them. It's perhaps indicative of a slightly flawed value system that somewhere along the line I let them go. Phil Hastin saved one of Fred's pieces. The work is childlike and primitive, written by an ancient person reaching out to a fading world.

But, he was creating real, live poetry in a place where creativity wasn't all that important and, by doing that, he became more than he really was.

Your Tender Smiles
*Just when the shadows fall, dear and
the gulls at evening rest
I'm left alone in my memories when
dreary dreams come to me
When the cold evening breeze drifts
along over the seas
The dark waters moan, and the
ripples croon
And the big golden moon shines in the sky
Then I'm thinking all the while of
your tender smiles
That makes the world so bright
I find my heart with you
I'll never forget the smiles and the
memories of you
When the night is dark and dreary
and the northern lights are gleaming
Then my heart is with you dear
in the home that's a heaven for me.*

Fred Foster

Norman Hodgson expected me to help Fred and I did. Most evenings when I was aboard I dried dishes, swabbed the galley floor and did other things for this aged and bent man who was filled with such an indomitable will. I never heard him speak of relatives; his life was veiled from those aboard the boat. He was gentle to me and is still etched in my mind at the half-door on the *Doris*, looking out, clutching a dishtowel and wiping at something, as he watched the wonders of an Alaskan summer roll by.

The Eagle runs under heavy weather after brailing an outside trap.

The 1940 salmon pack was a good one, about 180,000 cases of one-pound tall cans. With the cycle of the seasons, the procedure of shutting down for the winter began once again. The tenders dragged the trap frames to the head of the bay for winter storage. Most of the salmon pack had been sent south by steamer and there were only 33,000 cases left in the west warehouse to be shipped out on the next steamer. It was early September of a year that had exhibited a prodigious amount of rain and weather. Even the bay was rough that summer. The boats and tender crews had been battered and hard-used; it was a time for the licking of wounds. When one reached Seattle, he could sit before a winter wood fire and remember the adventures of brailing "outside." Some of the cannery crew had already been sent south on the steamer; we were rather "marking time" waiting for the return of the *North Sea* and the trip home.

For several days, at my mother's insistence, I had been shore bound helping her around our apartment and putting things away for the winter. Most of the tenders were out working, save for the little *Eagle* which was doing some "chores" close to the cannery. The little boat had labored hard that summer brailing, hull down, in tough weather beyond the Cape. Because of her size, she had to make a lot of trips, bringing the fish back in a too-small fish hold, thirteen thousand at a time. Phil Hastin skippered the *Eagle* as he did everything else—flawlessly. He had transformed the small tender from a garbage scow into a working tow boat, a little miracle in its way.

There was only a slight drizzle on that particular evening, a little respite from the almost constant downpour that had filled the summertime. After dinner in the Blue Room, Dad, Mother and I returned to the apartment over the store and settled in for the evening. I worked for awhile on a small model of the *Doris* I had started during the summer. I had put many hours in on her. She was almost finished now except for the rigging. I went to bed about ten, read a <u>Pacific Fisherman</u> for a few minutes then fell asleep.

Half an hour later I was awakened by a steam whistle blowing too many times. It was the cannery's emergency signal and something was wrong. By the time I ran into the front room, my dad was fully dressed and pulling on a pair of deck shoes. I had started to ask what was happening when there was a tremendous explosion next door and an immense fireball blasted out of the third floor of the cannery blowing the huge doors off the front of the building. Our apartment was only fifteen feet away. By this time my mother was up and I could hear the sounds of people running and shouting on the dock. The fire had started in the worst possible place, the web loft. That particular floor of the cannery building was filled with manila line, seine nets and trap-spiller nets. Some of the nets had been tarred while others had been treated with inflammable preservative coatings. There was a disaster in the making.

Dad and I rushed downstairs and ran around the front of the office. Already several men were unwinding a fire hose, rushing to pull it across the dock and aim it at the side of the tall cannery building adjacent to our second floor apartment. By this time, people were coming from all directions. Everyone's gaze was directed up at the third floor which showed no evidence of fire. The windows were dark and there was a faint hope that it was over. I recall turning toward Bill Lester, the storekeeper, and saying, "I guess it's out, Bill." In a high pitched voice he replied, "Hell Eddie, the building's so full of smoke we can't see the flames. The whole thing is going up ... everything ... everything!" He started to cry.

Water was now pouring from several fire hoses, but the streams of water barely reached the top of the building. For minutes the crowd grew and waited, some talking in muted voices, others just watching. Several frightened native women gathered around my mother asking what they could do. It was obvious, if the fire continued, our apartment would go immediately. I was amazed at my Mother's stoicism as she directed them to go upstairs, take out what clothes and valuables they could hold, and carry them to the native cabins which were far back on the beach and relatively safe. Watching her, I noticed she held in her hand a small eight-millimeter movie camera with which she would record the death of Port Althorp and the lifestyle which we had so enjoyed.

For several more minutes, as the hoses played a stream of water on the lower portions of the roof, a little hope remained. Then, with an audible gasp from the crowd, the flames broke out through the ridge pole and rafters of the building and, in an instant, all hope was gone. Everyone began rushing to do something; in minutes the dynamics of the group had changed from anxiety to survival. Dad instructed the cannery radioman standing beside him to send out a message to anyone listening that our situation was desperate. It was obvious that, without help, two hundred people were going to be stranded on a bitter cold and isolated Alaskan beach. The hazards and potential for loss of life had become enormous. Now, only a few minutes after the fire had started, the blaze had turned into a holocaust.

The flames immediately jumped the short distance between the flaming cannery building and our apartment. After running down the stairs with Dad at the onset of the fire, I never had the opportunity to go back again. I had the clothes on my back and a pair of sneakers; everything else was gone. Within twenty minutes the entire cannery building was engulfed in a roaring, searing pillar of flame. The second floor of the building was completely filled with heavy canning machines. When the building supports burned through, tons of red hot machinery on the second floor smashed downward carrying the first floor with it, sizzling and bubbling into the bay. As the building fell, it broke the timbers supporting the flume. No more water was available and one could only watch as the buildings and the entire dock became engulfed in flames.

Of huge concern was the oil dock some distance from the main cannery buildings. In addition to drums of gasoline and lubricating oil, a huge storage tank filled with twenty thousand gallons of diesel oil stood on the dock. If the oil dock caught fire, a tremendous inferno would follow. At the onset of the fire, Phil Hastin had rallied his crew and fired up the little *Eagle*. Now at the height of the fire, the tender was standing a dozen feet off the oil dock pouring sea water on the drums and tanks of gasoline and diesel with her deck pumps. She stood by all night pumping water on the steaming dock and was totally responsible for averting an even larger disaster. In addition to saving the oil dock, her action had saved a portion of the face of the main dock which was essential for evacuation of the cannery crew.

People did what they could as they retreated towards the safety of the beaches. Twenty or thirty high pressure oxygen and acetylene tanks were stored in the machine shop some little distance from the row of cannery buildings. When it became obvious that the fire was going to take everything, three of us rolled the tanks to the edge of the dock and shoved them over the side into the shallow water of the night's tide. Other drums of oil, grease and diesel were too heavy for us to move. As the fire reached them, they burned fiercely or blew up with a tremendous roar. There were minor explosions everywhere. The air was filled with cinders and burning particles. When buildings collapsed, sparks and bits of burning debris flew hundreds of feet into the sky and floated like fireflies in the upwelling of superheated air. With supports burned through, the main steam generating plant crashed down into the water leaving only two huge concrete pillars on which stood the charred remains of the plant's two generators. Someone had blown down the steam boiler, turned off the burners and set the safety valves open averting another cataclysmic explosion.

The warehouse was the last of the three large buildings to go. It burned rather more slowly, but the fire had traveled across the creosoted piling and dock timbers to undermine the building. When the foundation structure weakened from the flames, thirty-three thousand cases of salmon crashed, hissing into the bay. Some few hundred cases remained to be consumed by the fire. As they were heated, the cans blew up and flew through the night like small meteors leaving behind the smell of burned salmon and burned hope. The violence of the updraft of heated air created a circulating pattern which brought a cold wind across the scene. The forests and mountain side were illuminated by the flames, turning them a brilliant yellow green touched with blue-black patches of night shadows.

Fire is a noisome intruder. At times the sounds of the full-blown flames were overpowering, emitting an incessant roar that was punctuated by gigantic hissing sounds or ex-

Destruction of the cannery was devastating. In the few hours it burned, the fire reduced a fine operating facility and organization into ruin. This photograph shows the remains of the main power generator and its boiler. Decking and piling were almost totally consumed in the flames.

plosions of unknown things being consumed by the tremendous heat. The spectacle was awesome. People stood in small groups watching and saying nothing, seemingly unable to comprehend the destruction that was all about them. The rain, filled with ash and carried horizontally by the fire's wind, streaked the faces and clothes of everyone. No one escaped that; it was a universal.

Then it was over. The flames died down to a blaze here and there and thankfully the whole of the destruction was covered, for some little time, by the darkness of night and the falling rain. There was a desperate need for assistance now. Some few buildings above the tidelands had survived, two bunkhouses, a cook shack, some storage buildings and the small cabins occupied by the natives. These buildings were totally inadequate to house the number of people remaining even for a brief period. For the balance of the night, people sought refuge from the rain wherever they could. In an incredible stroke of good fortune, a passenger ship of The Alaska Steamship Company had been cruising near Juneau and immediately responded to the desperate cry for help. Under forced-draft they headed for the cannery indicating they would be there the following afternoon to remove as many persons as they could crowd aboard.

Dawn usually came with a gray wetness at Port Althorp. This morning was no exception. The cold light brought a smoldering scene of complete devastation. The oil dock and the main dock face, both saved by the *Eagle*, were the only things left. Of what had been the large dock area, only blackened piling remained. The concrete steam plant pillars, rising in the middle of the huge burned mass, were like headstones wreathed in a dirty, black haze. Lifted by the morning wind, gray ash swirled about covering the jet black of burned timbers, and painting the whole scene the color of the lowering sky. Here and there, wires, pipes, and strange bits of iron and steel poked up. These were the tools and machines we'd worked with and lived with. In many cases it was impossible to tell what they once were. What had been our apartment had fallen down in a charred mass on the rocky beach. Between tides I found the blackened barrel of my rifle, the remnants of a few pots and pans, and the twisted, burned steel box that had been my dad's radio. Beside that, there was nothing.

The steamer arrived that afternoon and evacuated everyone who wasn't absolutely essential to closing down whatever was left of the cannery. Food and supplies were dropped off for the skeleton crew that remained. The three of us stayed on for a week or two so that dad could supervise anything that might be left to do. It was a sad and depressing time. We took up temporary residence in a tiny room over the radio shack and ate at the small cookhouse; it was a far cry from the Blue Room. There was a deep and abiding depression about the place now. My dad had been deeply involved with the operation at Port Althorp for a number of years. The place was a source of pride to him and its loss was personally devastating. He carried on in his usual competent fashion attending to all details of the canning year and the subsequent fire, but there was a change in him, as if the fire had made him suddenly older. We had all lost more than a cannery that night.

A salvage company contracted to remove the cans of salmon, repackage them, and market the result as pet food. I worked for the contractor for a short time. Between the tides and amongst the blackened piling, we slogged about on the tidal rocks picking up thousands of discolored and burned cans; it was true stoop labor. We threw them into a cooler tray which was then lifted to the dock where they were stacked for shipment. It was a filthy job and I hated it. Overhead were the remnants of the burned docking from which ashes and soot mixed with ever falling rain steadily sifted down. This was a true learning experience; a far cry from the job of deckhand on the *Doris E*. I complained constantly and was saved from further abuse by the arrival of the *North Sea* which took us home. The contractor was later accused of relabeling and selling the reclaimed cans for other than the specified pet product. If such was the case, I could personally assure the purchaser that the cut-rate salmon they had selected was not only cooked, it was in fact well done.

Total devastation of the cannery. The building at the rear is on the oil dock, and filled with barreled gasoline and other inflammable fuels. It was saved and a huge explosion was averted by the heroic action of Phil Hastin, his crew, and the venerable Eagle.

The Years Between
1940-1947

Early in 1942 Kato Schwalling, who had been Second Engineer on the Doris E was killed near some damn worthless island in the Philippines.

It would be seven years before I came back to Alaska and to the boats which had been so much a part of my life. The decision to not rebuild the cannery came like a body-blow to my dad, one which he never got over. He was a man of great strength and composure and there was no railing against the decision or against any of those responsible. The fact was, there were only so many canneries, and they all had superintendents. He was out of a job, the responsibilities of which he had handled in an exemplary fashion. That kind of situation is always extremely difficult to handle—he handled it well.

I returned to high school and was sufficiently sensitive to develop a deep concern over the swirlings of war that were tugging at the heartstrings of the world. There seemed little doubt that America would soon be involved. France had fallen: England was besieged on every corner by the scourge of Nazi Germany, and, in righteous anger, young men were going to Canada to learn how to fly airplanes with guns on them. I was still playing street basketball and struggling to get a passing grade in Algebra. I heard periodically from Fred Foster, and my parents occasionally entertained long time friends from the old Port Althorp crew. Our ties to Alaska had grown weaker by circumstance but were never severed. Life seems much like a kaleidoscope. The turning of time twists the cardboard tube and brings to our lives novel and different patterns of intricate color and design. In the years ahead I would experience many new and changing interests, but always beside them, on a parallel track running into the future, would be the memory of my involvement with Alaska and the boats that had helped me grow up.

Until the Day Of Infamy on December seventh, 1941 had been a year of change. I worked that summer as a chauffeur for a wealthy Seattle family. Fortunately, they were unaware of my tendency to day-dream about Port Althorp while I was behind the wheel. I never ran into anything or bent a fender, but nothing was going to replace summertime and the *Doris E*. With a new Captain and crew, she was now hauling fish from the Port Althorp traps to the cannery located at Hawk Inlet. Norman Hodgson took another job and Phil Hastin went to work in a shipyard building and repairing mine sweepers and other smaller boats of war. He rose, as could be expected, to be foreman of the whole operation; Phil knew boats as few men do. The possibility of war had become an overshadowing presence. The Selective Service Act had been passed, and kids who were a little older than I were registering for the draft and going away to learn how to fight with something beside their fists.

There is no reason to dwell on Pearl Harbor. To those who were alive then, it was a day that galvanized the nation into a full and fateful determination to defeat the rotten regimes that were destroying freedom and the future of the world. Revisionist historians may wish to reconfigure that statement. I stand by it incontrovertibly, and am ready to do battle with those who might disagree. In the months of hardship and defeat which followed Pearl Harbor, Alaska and the people I had known there became deeply entwined with my life and thoughts. Late in the fishing season, on a trip from Hawk Inlet to brail traps in Icy Strait, the *Doris* attempted to tie up overnight at what was left of the Port Althorp dock. The night was dark and, since the *Doris* had wheelhouse engine controls, Claude Graham, the engineer, was on deck alone, ready with a mooring line. The approach was clumsy. When the *Doris* bumped the dock, Claude was thrown overboard and drowned. He was a fine and gentle man and an important part of my memories of the Port Althorp years. There was more sadness to come. Early in 1942 Kato Schwalling, second engineer on the *Doris E* was killed near some damn worthless island in the Philippines. He was barely older than I. Like the kids we were, we had fished together and joked together through Alaskan summers. I felt his death very keenly and feel it still in the retelling.

As 1942 dawned in the confusion and tumult of early war, my dad was recruited to go to Alaska and supervise the unloading of steamships containing construction materials for the Naknek Air Base. Because of shallow water in the area, materials for the construction of the air strip had to be off-loaded from freighters onto barges and thus transported to the air base site. It was a tough and frustrating responsibility, plagued by a shortage of tugs, barges, and people who knew what they were doing. Many Alaskan cannery tenders had been drafted into wartime service. Some of the larger and more powerful were pressed into towboat duty at Naknek and performed yeoman service; others remained on the fishing scene since the production of canned salmon was a wartime priority.

The weather around Naknek was constantly bad, and "bureaucratic molasses," in the form of confusion and indecision, was the diet of the times. In the war effort, everybody was trying to do the right thing at the right time and getting in each other's way. It didn't make much difference whether one were canning salmon, making tires, or building tanks, stress and confusion were a constant which permeated the lives of everyone involved. People did a lot of things they didn't want to do. Dad did not like flying but occasionally had to use aircraft in the fulfillment of his job responsibilities. On a winter trip in a small Spartan monoplane, the pilot attempted a landing on frozen Lake Iliamna and went through the ice on touchdown. The landing gear was badly bent and had to be pounded out cold on a local blacksmith's anvil. The machinery was bolted back together and sufficed for one subsequent take off and landing, then the little airplane was hauled off for professional repairs. The experience was a true adventure but failed to increase Dad's love of the air. My mother went to work for Foster and Kleiser, a local sign company. They undertook the task of camouflaging the huge Boeing airplane plant in south Seattle, covering it like a tent and making it look like a typical suburban neighborhood complete with cars and children's swing sets. It was a great effort which hindsight found totally unnecessary. Rumor mills had Japanese submarines off the entrance of Puget Sound. It was a time when everybody ran scared.

My dream was to become a Navy fighter pilot. That seemed to be a logical marriage of my compulsive affection for airplanes and boats. At age 17, I applied for enlistment in the flight training program of the Navy Air Corps. Completing their medical history form, I inadvertently checked the box indicating "Hay Fever." Some years before, in her incessant pursuit of the medical profession, my mother had convinced several renowned specialists that I was prone to hay fever and allergies. She had even convinced me. The Navy turned me down. Within an hour of this disappointment, and now completely cured of any nasal ailments, I stood in line at the Army Air Corps. Recruitment Center. I informed them that I was physically flawless and a born pilot. They took the bait and I was accepted for flight training.

There has been little in my life better than airplanes. The freedom of flight has been an elixir which I have pursued for over half a century. I have been pleased and proud of this compulsion. It has been with me so long that I believe I still see the sky with the wonder of a small child. I never want that to change. As a pilot, my war years were filled with adventure and the ongoing excitement of far places and intriguing pursuits. There was some genuine pain and loss of friends and crew-members, softened now by the years in between. I find it easier to remember the best part, when every day offered the opportunity to control some marvelous machine and enter another sphere of movement and exhilaration. Those times, for me, remain unforgettable.

During the war years there were some letters from home which bore unwelcome news. It was usually a folded newspaper clipping announcing that some friend or acquaintance was missing in action or dead. That happened all too often in those times. Dad didn't write frequently and, when he did, there was a reason. I can't recall whether I was in Bakersfield, Brazil, or Bangalore when I opened his letter telling me that my dear friend, Fred Foster, had died. There'd be no more epic poems issuing from his antique Underwood typewriter, and no more Alaskan summers passing by his galley "window-on-the-world." In another letter which I opened in another far place, I learned there would be no more mug ups in the galley of the *Doris E*. In the hands of strangers she had come in harm's way. Outside of Petersburg, she had caught fire and was run up on a gravel beach where she burned to the waterline. It was hard for me to imagine her gone. More than a boat had burned. She had been an intrinsic part of my growing years.

I returned home in January of 1946 after a year as a combat pilot in India and

China. There was an uncertainty in the return, a vague feeling of inadequacy, and a reticence and anxiety in tackling the job of adjusting to the future. The feeling was ill-defined and hovered about my mind just out of earshot. I never shared it with anyone, but I knew it was there and I lived with it. It was destined to get worse before it got better. A month or so after my return, Leif Buschmann contacted me about a charter air service he and a partner were starting. He indicated a desire for me to join them in what they hoped would be a commercial passenger and freight operation in the northwest and Alaska. Both Leif and his partner had limited time in the air and their undertaking seemed to me to be somewhat ambitious. He had previously talked to me about the small twin-engined aircraft they had purchased and, at Leif's request, I went with him to a small airfield east of Seattle on Mercer Island where their airplane was hangared.

I had flown that type of plane extensively and was totally unimpressed with its capabilities. I spoke with Leif at length regarding the limitations inherent in the airplane and at last realized that I was not spreading expertise, I was alienating a distant cousin. We parted as friends, but for several days I felt some discomfort at having dripped cold water on Leif's enthusiasm. My concern for the project was not unjustified. On April 26, 1946, Leif and his partner/co-pilot left Seattle on a passenger charter flight carrying four Ohio residents to their homes for Easter. The aircraft and all aboard vanished. The weather at the time of the flight was questionable and search flights for wreckage were conducted without results. On July 6, about two months later, a group of fishermen came upon the wreckage of the plane, screened by underbrush. It contained the bodies of Leif, his partner and his four passengers. The airplane had gone down on a heavily timbered mountainside, a scant hour's flying time from its departure point, and an eternity's distance from Ohio.

After the sorrow of Leif's fatal accident, the Summer and Fall of 1946 rolled by rather innocuously. I flew regularly in a reserve outfit and spent an intense and memorable afternoon at old Boeing Field trying to get the wheels down on a bad airplane. I did a lot of thinking after that near-miss. There seemed nothing negative about it. Instead, there was an intense thrill in the incident causing me to wonder if I would ever settle down and get over the need for that kind of thing. Then Asa happened. She was blond, Icelandic--a life-changing type of young woman and, although this is a story of boats and Alaska, it would be indefensible and stupid to leave her out. She was also bright, beautiful, and totally different from any woman I'd known before. In the sea of uncertainty I was crossing, she seemed the only thing I had to hold onto. She was very important.

The Season Of Forty-Seven

There was a shattering explosion and cracking amidships; in an instant everyone aboard realized the blow had stove-in her planking and broken her ribs.

By January of 1947, my fiscal situation had become badly eroded; it was time I started thinking about gainful employment. There were two important reasons for this seemingly impulsive concern; first, I was broke, second, I felt a genuine need to return to Alaska. I recall the feeling now as almost a homing instinct, a demand to get back to some kind of pre-war root structure so I could begin growing again. There had been so much security and joy for me there, it seemed only natural to want to return. But, there was another sadness to be encountered and another thread to be broken. On February 13th. 1947, the *North Sea*, southbound, struck a rock in Seaforth Channel near Bella Bella B. C. Attempts to float her were unsuccessful and for years she would lie pilloried there, rusting away on a fog shrouded rock pile. A few days after the stranding of the *North Sea*, I went to the offices of the Nakat Packing Corporation in Seattle and asked for a job. I entered the Nakat office with a rather high degree of confidence, feeling I knew something about boats and Alaska. Alas, I wasn't hired for my high degree of marine expertise, I was hired because Eigel Buschmann was General Superintendent of the company and he wanted to help me out. Norman Buschmann would also work for Nakat at the Waterfall Cannery that summer, and I feel that Eigel was pleased that Norman and I were friends and would be working fairly closely together. Being the same age and pretty footloose, Norman and I had done some post-war drinking together and got along well. Waterfall would be a lot more fun with him there.

I started work one early morning in March when I reported to Maritime Shipyard not far from the Ballard Locks. All the Nakat Packing Corporation tenders wintered at the Maritime yard. I was assigned as deckhand on the *Frederick C*. She was named for Frederick C. Johnstone an early salmon cannery pioneer who at one time owned the Waterfall Cannery. I would rather have believed she carried that name in memory of Frederick C. Buschmann, who had died in the sinking of the seine boat *Eidsvold* the year my parents had married. The *Frederick C* was built

about 1918. She was a good boat, somewhat of a compromise between a towboat and fish hauler, having a good sized fish hold forward with a capacity of about 20,000 fish. As such, she had some of the advantages and the disadvantages that are inherent in any compromise. She was of a rather handsome configuration with a smaller main deckhouse and a second-story bridge and wheelhouse. She had been built about ten years earlier than the *Doris E*, and lacked some of the modernity and "slickness of line" of the newer boat. The *Frederick* stood taller and was less wide amidships, thus she was given to rolling a bit in a beam sea. She had somewhat the air of a "dowager" about her, sort of drawn up, imperious and unconcerned. She was heavy built and heavy powered but, as I soon found out, it was her crew that set her apart.

The *Frederick* was skippered by Henry Gundersen, a red-haired, articulate Norwegian who was probably about forty at the time. Henry was a no-nonsense skipper with a dry sense of humor. He ran a very tight ship. Norman Vaara, mate on the *Frederick*, was a tall, raw-boned kid who had been early on his own. He had operated a bulldozer during the building of the Alaskan highway, honing a natural affinity to work with heavy equipment. He handled a boat with the same skill and finesse he displayed when he played the guitar and told jokes in a magnificent Norwegian dialect suitable for professional entertaining. He and Gundersen, skilled and competent, admired and complemented each other. It was plain to see that Vaara would soon have his own command. Bob Erling was the cook. He was about my age, full of fun, and completely competent in the galley which he despised. His father was chief cook at the Waterfall Cannery and had taught him how to cook, but not how to enjoy it. In spite of that problem, Bob never served a bad meal. Virgil Schmoetzer was the young Assistant Engineer. Virgil was extremely tall, very bright, and so lean he had a scarecrow look about him. He constantly hitched at the belt line of his jeans in an ongoing effort to keep his pants up. Virgil moved fast and smiled at everything. If he had an idiosyncrasy, it was the fact that he incessantly hummed the melody of the "Wabash Cannonball." I was soon convinced it was the only song he had ever learned.

Then there was Leonard, the Chief Engineer. At about fifty, he was a nice man and the oldest person on the crew. I never knew from where Leonard had come. He was a "new hire" with little boat experience and a huge handicap; Leonard could not learn the engine room signals. The *Frederick* had no wheelhouse controls. In such a vessel, the required engine speeds and direction of propeller rotation were relayed from the wheelhouse to the engineer in the engine room through a series of bells and jingles, the response to which must be accurate and correct. Leonard's failure to grasp the meaning of these jingling bells was a problem seeking an immediate solution. Such an ineptitude might well send the *Frederick* under a dock at full speed ahead, dismasting her, and sweeping her clean above the railings. Henry Gundersen was a tolerant if demanding skipper, but when asking the engine room for reverse...he meant reverse! If he didn't get it, he turned into a raging Norwegian fury whose demeanor was a terrible thing to see. This whole situation was compounded by the fates. The *Frederick* was powered by a handsome Atlas Imperial diesel engine, unfortunately it was direct reversible. I have already explained the dangers lurking in that system of engine reversing. With Leonard aboard, Henry was faced with the necessity to worry about two things: the engine's inherent capacity to fail to start in reverse, and the equally deep concern that Leonard might misunderstand the bell signal ordering him to put the engine in reverse. This distressed Gundersen and made him lose sleep.

After we had bounced off a couple of docks, an act followed by screaming from the skipper about the engineer's ancestry, we practiced. Henry took the *Frederick* out in the bay where there was ample room for error and put Leonard through his paces many times. This entailed signaling for full reverse from a variety of different situations. Sometimes Leonard got it right, but not always. The situation was somewhat akin to having a small rock in the crew's collective shoe, you thought about it all the time. When we were approaching a dock, I never stood by a forward line without mentally preparing myself to run aft and throw myself down on the deck should Leonard miss his signals. It promised to be an exciting summer.

With the passage of a few days, it became apparent that working on the *Frederick* was to be a rich and unforgettable experience. Almost immediately the crew jelled into a solid and cohesive working team. On this boat, just being aboard seemed a privilege. With the exception of Leonard and his problem, the crew was totally competent, industrious and compatible. There were many things involved in getting a tender ready to go north in the spring. The boat was totally painted inside and out enriching the patina that had developed from countless spring times before. Decks were scrubbed and painted, and the engine was prepared for a summer of constant and demanding operation. Provisions, tools, engine materials and personal gear had to be put aboard and stowed properly in the correct spot. There was a great deal of territoriality in the placing of items aboard a working tow boat.

Space was limited and it was essential, in the case of emergency, that one be able to retrieve specialized tools or equipment in the fastest possible time. The cook's allotted space was especially inviolate, as was the engineer's. In short, "Nobody put nothin' in anybody else's place." It was a rule to live by.

Working ashore was the same as working at sea. Although tied to the dock in a quiet waterway, mug ups in the galley were an intrinsic and inviolate part of each day. They included coffee, goodies, an assessment of progress made in readying the boat, and a plan for the completion of future tasks. There was always a studied informality here, but the obvious need for communication was fulfilled time and again over the galley table. Henry and Norman both preceded work demands with such openers as; "Maybe we better," or, "I think we ought to." That was an easy way to receive orders, and provided the incentive for one to do as he was told. Each individual had responsibilities to fulfill and was expected to do so expeditiously, with minimal supervision, and without complaint. In this manner, the small society was welded into an interdependent group that could function with effectiveness while tied at the dock or in a heavy and dangerous sea. The process was as effective as any I had seen before or have witnessed since.

Word came down that our first task was to tow the company gear scow from Seattle to the cannery at Waterfall on Prince of Wales Island, a distance of about 650 miles, give or take a few twists and turns. The Nakat gear scow was a virtual duplicate of the one which had served Port Althorp. It was a massive contraption, blunt, unwieldy, high sided and a heavy tow. With a towing speed of only three or four knots, not withstanding any adversity, it was easy to see that the job would require about eight to ten days. We were then to return to Seattle and, after reloading, proceed north again with a load of cannery supplies.

With a little extra effort required to meet the deadline of March 15th, the *Frederick C* was made ready for the tow trip north. On the day before our scheduled departure, Bob, our cook, asked me to help him hang a large section of beef from a huge meat hook on the front of the gear scow which was moored close to us at Maritime Shipyard. This really didn't make any sense; it would, of course, be rotten before we got to Waterfall a week and a half later. I asked him why he was wasting a nice cut of beef like that and was told we would be eating it after we got to the cannery. I told him if he thought I was going to eat a piece of meat that had been hanging out on a scow rotting for a couple of weeks he was "crazy as hell!" He, in turn, suggested I "stuff it," and advised me that I could open a can of Vienna sausage if I didn't like what he prepared. That seemed the end of the controversy.

The afternoon before we departed, another incident of interest occurred. They brought our "ship stores" aboard. The crew had chipped in to purchase two cases of Norwegian Aquavit, a delightful booze that was strong enough to split one's skull. Since it was tax free, it was delivered by a Customs Official and duly locked and sealed in the small lazarette hatch in the afterdeck of the *Frederick*. We would enjoy it only at the pleasure of the circumstance and the Skipper and, sure as hell, not during working hours. The Aquavit was, "a sauce for the summer," and never caused a problem. Our departure was preceded by an informal "shore party" attended by the wives and girlfriends of the crew. Since we would return in two or three weeks, partings were only a slight trauma. As I recall, there were few, if any, tears. Even though there seemed an adventure in the offing, I felt no joy in saying good-bye to Asa. A few beers and sandwiches were consumed followed by some handshakes, hugs, and kisses. Then, there was the leaving and the journey had begun.

The gear scow was an ugly tow. She wallowed and veered from side to side until, through trial and error, Henry Gundersen discovered the proper length of tow line to let out. After that she tracked a little better, but all the way to Waterfall she towed like an untrained dog looking for a fire hydrant. The scow had no grace about her. The square forward end of her pushed tons of water aside in her slow progress and she tended to "hobbyhorse" in the slightest swell. At least she was a couple of hundred yards astern where we didn't have to look at her all the time. With a

fair tide, six hours of running time put us abeam of Whidbey Island in a gathering darkness. With the scow on our leash, we had covered a whopping twenty-five miles since departing the Ballard Locks. No speed records were being set. A slight swell rolled down through the Strait of Juan de Fuca, and poked us in the port side and the *Frederick* rolled gently in response. Our course would twist and turn through the San Juan and Gulf Islands then head just east of north through the Strait of Georgia. Dinner was prepared in the galley which now exuded the warmth and security of a haven in a sea of darkness. The cohesion of the boat and crew was a shared thing, an entity which one could feel and savor. At dinner I was assigned the watch from midnight till four in the morning. I had put a new, blue-ticked, mattress on my upper bunk in the forecastle and was anxious to try it out. With the sound of the engine rumbling on the other side of the bulkhead, I turned in early, and went immediately to sleep.

A night wheel watch has always been my favorite time at sea. Unless one has experienced this privilege, such preference may be a hard thing to understand. I was now equipped with the knowledge and confidence that made me secure in handling the boat at night. In my Air Corps training, I had been extensively schooled in celestial and dead reckoning navigation, chart orientation, and radio procedures. There is little difference between the navigation techniques used in an aircraft or those used on a boat; a trackless sky is about the same as a trackless sea. Postwar radios were eons ahead of the huge black transmitter and receiver which had taken up so much space in the wheelhouse of the *Doris E*. The radio on the *Frederick*, in contrast, was a small compact unit on a shelf at the rear of the wheelhouse. The war had changed a lot of things. This radio didn't always smell like it was hot, and it always worked. Although the *Frederick* was not equipped with them, automatic direction finders, flasher depth sounders and radar had been developed. Even a primitive loran locator was available for larger sea-going vessels. All these electronic boxes provided a partial answer to the ever present question, "Where am I and where am I bound?" The elation I found during a night wheel watch had nothing to do with the electronics or technology the war had devised. These sophisticated ornaments were out of our reach. I relished a night watch because of the "world" one entered when he ascended the ladder to the bridge.

It would have been unthinkable to stand a watch without at least a "beginning coffee." On "double decker" tenders I always used one hand to climb a rung or two up the bridge ladder, place the cup on the upper deck, then finished the climb to the bridge with two hands on the rungs. The coffee was then retrieved from the deck and the inboard hand could be used to open the wheelhouse door.

As usual, no matter the cannery tender or its age, wheel house doors always stuck and were always cursed, I have mentioned the protocol of "receiving the wheel" from the previous watch keeper. In this prologue, there was a time allotted for short conversation and information about heading and location and a period of minutes for the oncoming watch to check the chart by a carefully guarded light. A swig or two of very hot coffee, followed by an, "OK, I got it." signaled the formalized assumption of responsibility. With the departure of the previous watch keeper, the magic began.

With assumption of the "night wheel," I always experienced an awakening and keening of the senses. In minutes, even on the darkest of nights, visual acuity improved to that point where images became defined and recognizable. Since we were traveling through a "peopled area," lights on shore decorated the sides of our journey while lights from navigational aids delineated the pathway ahead. Night smells in the wheelhouse were marvelous mixtures of coffee, faint cigarette smoke, a whisp of diesel fume and the indigenous scent of wood, brass, lubricating oil and rope. A warmth always came from somewhere, I was never cold on watch. The night and boat were alive with the vibration and the sea-motions of our "way," while the whole of this was wrapped in a soothing mantle of darkness and aloneness I have found nowhere else on earth.

In retrospect, a night watch always freed my mind from the bondage of daytime thinking. Engine sounds and the creaks and groans of a vessel underway faded into an inconsequential background that became nothing. Time was no factor. Thoughts, hopes, and dreams could flash back recalling the past or race ahead to encompass the possibilities of the future. The impact of conversation or personal interaction was blissfully absent and, for these short hours, aloneness was something to treasure. The red compass light gave only faint illumination to interior surroundings and did nothing to hamper the view ahead which was often silvered by a moon or ambient light. Other vessels told of their directional intentions and encumbrances by means of navigation and towing lights while beacons, buoys, and an occasional lighthouse vividly set apart the pathway stretching out before us.

There was always a tall oak stool in every wheelhouse and, like the one on the *Doris*, this one's legs were strongly cross-wired so one could tilt it back with complete confidence. On long wheel watches, I sat on this stool and steered the boat with my feet resting on the steering spokes. This was a universal posture practiced by all. Effective steering was a learned skill. The novice always over-steered, cranking the wheel back and forth too far and too fast, leaving a zigzag wake astern which indelibly stamped the steersman as incompetent. With practice, the yawing of the boat could be anticipated and checked with only a spoke or two's movement that saved energy and minimized the compass swing; thus, assuring a better and more accurate course.

Wheelhouse windows were of a universal type. Like those on the *Doris*, the *Frederick's* were opened and closed by means of a leather belt. If one became drowsy, there was an instant cure. Merely lower the window a few inches, and the incredible sharpness and clarity of the night wind would bring one wide awake in seconds. The gear scow was never out of mind. When opposing swells were encountered by the boat and the tow, the *Frederick* would be "brought up short" as if she'd been lassoed by a rubber band. There would be an awkward lurching backward, requiring repositioning of the feet by all those awake, and producing an unpleasant awakening for all those asleep. Then the inevitable progress would begin again. An obvious responsibility was to periodically check the scow by means of a large spotlight mounted above the wheelhouse and controlled by a brass wheel extending down through the overhead. Each time the light picked up the scow far astern, I could see Bob's side of beef swinging wildly back and forth soaked by spray and turning green. I thought to myself, "no one was going to eat that and live."

Our progress continued northward at a snail's pace, it was as though one were "walking" the journey. Always before I had come this way on the *North Sea*, quite literally a "racehorse" when compared with the lumbering *Frederick C* and her tow. Our reduced speed, amounting to little more than a stroll, created a time warp, a panoramic window through which we could view the singular magnificence that lined our route.

We passed through the confines of Discovery Passage and Johnstone Strait, the shores of which were cloaked in endless spruce and fir forests which rose from the water's edge and soared unbroken to the timberline. The greens and blues of this "timber carpet" were crowned with snow-filled granite crags weeping small waterfalls which, in turn, cascaded down their faces like bits of lace. There was life everywhere, and every turn in our passage disclosed some new and unexpected beauty. Deer could be spotted on the beach. With heads held high, their ears examined the constant beat of the unobtrusive diesel. We were far away and posed no threat. Eagles and hawks, seeking prey, circled the higher cliff areas in endless expectation. The waters of Johnstone Strait teemed with killer whales and other sea life which had been rotating in the chain of their existence for a million years and more. I had been this way before. In rare instances, small, half remembered dwellings and anchored, ill-kept, boats dotted a far cove or inlet and signaled the lasting presence of some hardy isolationist. But, signs of habitation were the exception to the rule; there had been little change in the years between. The overwhelming fare of our passage remained virginal, untouched, unsullied and unforgettable.

Although the pace of work aboard the boat was slow, it was also steady. There was always something to be done when one was not on wheel watch. I spent two days cleaning out a small paint locker which had been in a disreputable state for years. Some painting was left to be done in the engine room and forecastle, a few provisions were left to be stowed and there were lines to be spliced and letters to be written. No one stood by a hard and fast rule as to the particular tasks in which he should be involved. There was a common assumption of responsibility. If help was needed in the engine room, the deck crew stood by. Conversely, if deck chores were of a major concern, the engine room crew pitched in to help. Henry absolutely insisted on one unique instance of shared responsibility. If the boat were to be maneuvered in tight quarters, Virgil was to assist Leonard in interpreting the engine room signals. Virgil was good at it. We all felt better after that.

The miles and time reeled slowly by in a constantly changing, always enticing pattern of primal loveliness. After a relatively flat passage through Queen Charlotte Sound, we continued north, finally passing the spot op-

posite Bella Bella where the *North Sea* had run aground. It was a sad sight to see her exposed there naked and defenseless. I was truly moved by the sight. We saw she was abandoned, bent over the rocks, with her bow high out of the water and covered with a motley sea growth. It was evident that there would be no saving her; she would be reclaimed by the sea. Beside a steel hull, many of the happiest moments of my childhood had hit the rocks with her. Even my favorite viewing spot on the fantail would be nearly awash in a heavy flood tide. At our speed it took a long time to pass her. It was like looking too long at an open casket. I was glad when we turned the corner at Campbell Island and lost her from sight.

We approached Dixon Entrance with some justifiable foreboding. As usual, this would be the toughest segment of the journey. At our speed the crossing would require 10 to 12 hours, and we had already received an invitation to the party in the form of waves and wind. By the time we cleared Rose Point, we could look toward the open Pacific to the west and guess what was coming. We really didn't cross Dixon Entrance, we went through it! In weather like this, one held onto something to stay alive and hoped for the best. The overture began with pots and pans crashing to the floor and the sound of Bob's cussing, cutting through the overhead, transcended the noise of the storm. All over the boat things crashed, thudded, and rolled. There would be hours of this ahead. With plenty of line out astern, the wallowing scow threw tons of water over her blunt bow with every wave. At times Bob's beef was totally lost, immersed in solid sea water. But after every assault, like the Star Spangled Banner, the green side of beef still waved. There was not much cheering about that. The *Frederick* took the battering well, but after a couple of hours of thrashing, Norman Vaara became concerned about some sacks of flour stored under the forecastle ladder and asked me to move them. By that time we were taking green water over the bow and the forecastle head doors were not all they should be.

I left the wheelhouse and stepped into a brutally cold wind filled with sea spray and storm sounds. The boat was rolling heavily as I made my way down the ladder and, by the time I reached the forecastle head, I was soaking wet. I opened the doors and, before descending, closed them tightly after me. It was of little use. Every wave coming over the bow sent water cascading through the closed doors and down the ladder onto the ten sacks of flour stacked on the sole of the forecastle. There was nothing to do but move them all to a drier spot. At this point I noticed that two of my crew mates were prostrate in their bunks. Their condition could only be described as "sicker than hell!" With the darkness, the smell, and the task at hand, the forecastle was a place where no one would actually choose to be; it was a shambles. The door to a medicine chest on the aft bulkhead had flown open and the chest had disgorged a combination of glass bottled merchandise which fractured on the sole and filled the bilges with an aroma that is better imagined than described. Ankle deep salt water, filled with floating things, sloshed back and forth as the boat rolled from side to side. Somebody's blanket had fallen into the sodden mass. By that time, the owner didn't care. By the time the flour sacks were stacked in an empty bunk out of harm's way,

Waterfall Cannery on Prince of Wales Island

my physical condition had been downgraded from questionable to critical. It was all I could do to crawl into my bunk and hold on until one of three things occurred: either the storm subsided, we reached shelter, or I died. I stayed in my bunk until we passed the blessed barrier of Cape Muzon and Dall Island and came upon the smoother waters of Cordova bay. Such was my reintroduction to Dixon Entrance. Regretfully, it would not be our last confrontation, but it would be our last one in ill health. We'd gotten our sea legs the hard way. There were fifty quiet miles to go to reach Waterfall. Just time enough for several of us to rejoin the living and clean up and dry out the forecastle, a very unwelcome task.

Waterfall Cannery was tucked into a small bight on Ulloa Channel, a very narrow and, at times, exciting body of water. We later referred to a portion of the Channel as the "Skookumchuck." Great masses of water swept through it on tidal changes, a little like the sand in an hour glass. In a strong ebb or flood tide, the Skookumchuck was very much akin to a narrow, fast moving, river filled with massive whirlpools and incredible tidal bores which swept its length like a set of stairs. Steering a bare boat through this maelstrom was a constant adventure; with a heavy tow, it was an impossibility.

We waited for slack water, then moved carefully on up the channel, circled gently to our right, and moored the boat and scow at the dock. The gear scow had been a long hard tow and, with its release, there was the feeling an unwelcome task had been completed. Without the encumbrance and, to the joy of everyone, the *Frederick* had regained her freedom as she moved easily and quickly about her few remaining chores. Waterfall Cannery was an efficient and beautifully kept salmon plant, probably the finest such installation in Alaska. Its buildings were massive, of recent construction, and the facilities and the company's methods of operation were the best to be found anywhere.

For its supply of salmon, Waterfall operated nine fish traps and processed large amounts of seine and troll fish producing some of the largest salmon "packs" in Alaska.

On our arrival, Bob Erling our cook, took down the large beef quarter which had decorated the front of the gear scow all the way from Seattle. I jokingly helped him carry it on board the *Frederick* with every expectation it would be thrown overboard. The outside was green and covered with a layer of accumulated salt as hard as a brick. Surprisingly, a fellow sailor, Richard Dana, in his book <u>Two Years Before The Mast</u>, had mentioned salt beef, the curse of the early mariner. One hundred and sixty-five years before our journey from Seattle he had quoted an ancient poem about the bad meat that came to the table of the common seaman.

*"Old Horse! Old Horse!
What brought you here?'
'From Sacarap' to Portland Pier
I've carted stone this many a year;
Till, killed by blows and sore abuse,
They salted me down for sailors' use
The sailors they do me despise;
They turn me over and damn my eyes;
Cut off my meat, and scrape my bones,
And send me down to Davy Jones.*

With a large butcher knife, Erling removed the crusted layer revealing an inside that was as fresh and inviting as any cut of meat might be. It looked as though Dana might be in error. Bob cooked a portion that night and I ate my share and more. With the skipper's approval, the dinner was enhanced by a bottle of Aquavit. A little bit of the Norwegian whiskey went a long way in helping the crew forget about the accursed gear scow and the crossing of Dixon Entrance. For a week we ate the beef: diced, sliced, broiled, and boiled, then finished up with sandwiches. It was delicious; I had learned something.

For a few days we did some pre-season odd jobs about the cannery, towed some trap logs from a small mill nearby, and re-provisioned for the trip south. We left the cannery on an early afternoon unencumbered by the gear scow and free as a bird. There was a mandatory stop at the little town of Craig some fifteen miles north east of the cannery. Arriving there, the crew trudged up the slight hill at the end of "Main Street" and entered the town's finest bar: Lib and Jessie's Cocktail Lounge. This watering hole would become a favorite weekend spot during the canning season. It was owned by two delightful women who came to regard the crew of the *Frederick C* as their own. For some little time the crew drank beer while Norman Vaara played his guitar and some songs in his famous Norwegian dialect. It was a memorable afternoon and evening. After dinner at a local restaurant, we retired to the boat pretty well loaded and blissfully happy with the lot of a cannery tender crew member. Fortunately, no one fell off the float. The next morning at dawn we headed back for Seattle. We passed Waterfall on the fly and, as I remember, hit the Skookumchuck on a roaring ebb tide and raced through it like a torpedo boat. Seven or eight hour's running time put us opposite Cape Muzon, the beginning of Dixon Entrance. Ironically, the crossing was like a millpond as was the remainder of the trip south. After an absence of a little over two weeks we tied up at Maritime Shipyards. My first stop was at a pay phone; I called Asa at the University of Washington Dorm to tell her I was home.

For the next two weeks the *Frederick's* crew worked on company boats in the Seattle shipyard. Painting chores required most of our time, but there was also engine work, the major task of an oil change, and the securing of provisions for the return trip north. All these activities filled up the balance of our eight-hour days. Three cannery tenders and two power scows served Waterfall for the season of 1947. Best of the cannery tenders was the *Quaker Maid*, a truly beautiful work boat styled in the manner of a seine boat but much larger. She had a flying bridge and was a dual purpose vessel, working as a tender and fish hauler in the summer in Alaska and doubling as an off-shore seiner out of California in the winter time. The *Quaker Maid* was built in 1935 and was perhaps the last of a type of Alaskan cannery tender to be constructed. She was powered by a huge Washington Estep diesel engine and was a work boat of beauty, class and power.

The Quaker Maid, flagship of the Nakat Packing Corporation tender fleet.

The Golden West

The *Golden West* was a typical fish-hauling tow boat, with a single level deck. She was heavily built, but possessed little style. She would do what was expected of her and probably, not a lot more. It was certain that she would never win, place, or show in a boat beauty contest. The *Rolfy* and The *Eigel B.* were power scows, and performed exclusively as fish-haulers. The power scow was essentially what the name implied, a scow with a propulsion engine and a two level house aft which served as crew quarters, engine room and galley. The bows on these craft were somewhat "boat shaped," but lacked the beauty and finesse of a conventional boat hull. In a walled and compartmented area forward, these scows could haul about 30 to 35 thousand fish and, while surely utilitarian, they were square, boxy, and unattractive. Contraptions such as these had no soul. I always felt they were something that should be towed behind a real boat.

The two weeks we spent in the shipyard passed too quickly and it was again time for a good-bye to wives, girlfriends and Seattle. These farewells would last for six or seven months and were accompanied by a much greater degree of emotion than that displayed at the last parting. Asa was there. Unlike the previous farewell we joked and laughed only a little, nothing seemed too funny. When it finaly came time to let the mooring lines go, she turned and walked away crying. It was very difficult for me to leave her.

The *Frederick* was loaded with supplies but blissfully, this time, there was no scow dragging behind her. We made a quick and uneventful trip north, and became immediately involved in the frenetic activity surrounding preparation for a salmon canning season. There were frame logs to be towed, trap frames to be completed, towed to location, and anchored, and a hundred other boat chores which filled our days. Although there was plenty of rain, there seemed an absence of the weather bitterness I'd remembered at Port Althorp. The *Frederick* had grown into a performing entity under the leadership of Henry Gundersen and Norman Vaara. I believe we all took pride in the performance of the boat and the job we were doing. Living conditions were excellent with fine food, hot showers and a crew that had developed a genuine sense of cohesion and friendship. The cannery administration, from the superintendent on down, was "boat oriented" and understanding of the challenges and difficulties inherent in the operation of a cannery tender. Waterfall smacked a bit of Camelot, a marvelous place to work. Norman Buschmann was serving as mate on the *Quaker Maid*. When both boats were in the cannery at the same time, we spent a good deal of time together. Norman, like his father, handled a fishing boat with a tremendous degree of aplomb. Anyone just standing on the flying bridge of the *Quaker Maid* looked like a God from Neptune's Kingdom. It wasn't the man at the wheel, it was the inherent beauty of the vessel.

In the space of a couple of weekends, to pass time, we resurrected an old speed boat and got it running. I built an "aquaplane" out of the bin-boards from an old fish scow and, with Norman at the controls of the speed boat, I rode the aquaplane before a cheering group of idle cannery workers and native seine boat crews. I nearly froze, but our performance was a triumph. Wherever Norman might be, we still hold joint claim to the role of producers of the only "Aquacade Follies" ever held in the fish-gurry waters of Waterfall, Alaska.

Toward the end of May I retrieved a cast off copy of the Seattle Times from a cannery garbage can. The front page bore a fascinating item covering a narrowly averted tow boat tragedy which had occurred only weeks before. This particular marine happenstance involved the *Hercules*, a large Seattle tug boat belonging to the Puget Sound Tug and Barge Company. The towboat circle was a rather close-knit fraternity and though a cannery tender could scarcely lay claim to total "tug boat stature," we still felt a kinship with these handsome boats that were nearly twice our size and ten times as powerful. I was well acquainted with the company and the boat and the story, I believe, bears retelling.

The battleship Oklahoma had been sunk during the attack on Pearl Harbor. Raised from the mud and righted toward the middle of the war, the bare hull remained moored for several years near the spot of its sinking. Because of hull deterioration, the decision to auction her for scrap was finally made. In December of 1946 she was purchased as salvage by the Moore Drydock Company of Oakland, California, and two ex-navy tugs, the *Hercules* and the *Monarch* were sent to Pearl Harbor to tow the floating hulk back to Oakland for dismantling. Huge and powerful, these ocean-going tugs were 112 feet long, and each was equipped with a mammoth diesel engine of 1100 horsepower. Just after the first of May, the two tugs left Oahu and began the tow. May 17, 1947 found them 850 miles northwest of Oahu making fair way in calm seas. In total darkness, at about 1:30 in the morning, the hull of the *Oklahoma* suddenly capsized and, for unexplained reasons, began to sink in fifteen thousand feet of water.

The Hercules and Monarch were attached to the rapidly sinking *Oaklahoma* by 1400 feet of 1 3/4 inch steel towing cable of tremendous strength and, as the hulk went down, it began pulling the tugs after her. The force exerted by the sinking hull was enormous. The tugs were pulled backward at such speed that their engines were turned in reverse and a major disaster was in the making. The towing cable on the *Monarch* at last pulled off the towing drum, releasing her and sparing her from certain sinking, but the *Hercules*, with her towing drum "dogged down," and locked in position, appeared doomed. She was being pulled rearward at an estimated 25 to 30 knots when the immense towing winch was suddenly torn from her after deck and careened off the stern taking the aft bulkheads with it. She was released at last from the threat of being dragged down three miles to the bottom, but she was still in major trouble. Her engine room was completely flooded and the stern had sustained major damage. Through ingenuity and teamwork, the crews of both vessels labored to effect repairs and the two tugs made a miraculous return to San Francisco for emergency repairs. News of this tow boat accident passed quickly among the tender fleet and served as a graphic example of the hazards involved when towing objects which might suddenly sink. After this incident, the *Frederick's* winch was never "dogged down'" and we made sure the towing cable could be quickly released.

During the course of the season our primary responsibility was to brail traps and supply trap watchmen with the essentials of life. Obviously these duties had to be performed in all kinds of weather. The *Frederick* was an ideal boat for the purpose. In rough weather or when brailing outside traps we could not handle a scow, thus we loaded fish directly into the hold. In fair weather and seas, we could carry and brail into a scow and carry about thirty thousand fish per load. It was our business to get the fish out of the trap and into the cannery as quickly as possible regardless of the weather, the tides, or any other vagary of nature. We took great pride in our performance but, at times, the job wasn't easy. Nakat had several traps to the Westward, literally on the open sea. These locations were great for fishing but were exposed, at times, to savage weather and sea conditions. Brailing such traps was often dangerous and always an adventure.

About mid-season we set out to brail a trap off Noyes Island close to Cape Addington. The trap was one of our regular locations to brail, but the weather was "dicey" with a rising wind and a nasty sea. We were running light and Henry did a masterful job of laying the *Frederick* along the head log. She was made fast with fenders down, and it was our intention to empty the trap as quickly as possible and "get the hell out of there." The brailing was going well when suddenly someone shouted "Look Out!" I grabbed a nearby shroud and turned seaward to see an immense wave bearing down on us at tremendous speed. When the wave hit us, it lifted the *Frederick* straight up, rolled her violently to port, then smashed her down against the head

The Frederick, down by the bow.

log with stunning force. There was a shattering explosion and cracking amidships; in an instant everyone aboard realized the blow had stove-in her planking and broken her ribs. With a fish hold half full of salmon we were in trouble.

Henry shouted for us to throw off the mooring lines and we pulled away from the now deadly head log at full speed ahead. When clear of the fish trap by a hundred yards, he rang down the engine room to neutral-idle. Someone had raced after the heavy iron bilge pump bar and we immediately began to pump out the fish hold by means of a huge manual bilge pump on the aft deck. We couldn't see the damage since the level of brailed fish was above the point of impact. She had been lifted high and the head log had struck her very low in the turn of the bilge. There was no question the damage was serious. We turned toward home at half speed ahead not wanting to stress the hull anymore than absolutely necessary. Our continued manual pumping seemed to prevent any water rise in the fish hold and indeed the pump flow became smaller and required only intermittent pumping. In two hours, we were alongside the fish dock and unloaded immediately. It was as everyone expected, the damage was extensive. Two of her immense ribs had been fractured and some planking cracked but she remained sound taking only a little water through the damaged planks. Repairs had to be undertaken immediately.

The closest boat repair facility with a "ship ways" large enough to pull the *Frederick* out of the water was located in Ketchikan. We made a slower than usual run down Cordova Bay, turned the corner at Cape Chacon in slack water, then headed northwest for forty-five miles arriving at Ketchikan in the early evening. The next morning we were hauled out for repairs which would require a week's stay in Ketchikan. For a young cannery tender crew it was a miraculous bonanza. We slept and ate on the boat while she was under repair and spent the days of our enforced idleness wondering at the blessings which had befallen us. Needless to say, our pay went on while we had absolutely nothing to do. We visited curio shops, shot the breeze with boat yard workers, winked and smiled at pretty tourist girls in downtown Ketchikan, drank beer, and regularly visited Dolly's chintz-laden whorehouse on Creek Street, which we always called "Crick Street."

It is my understanding that Dolly's little crib has now been "refined," and is euphemistically referred to as Dolly's Historic Museum. It is apparently now visited by hordes of contemporary tourists who rush off cruise ships to giggle and whisper of its notorious past. I am proud to say that when I visited Dolly's place in those wonder years at Waterfall, it was a full fledged, operational, viable, dyed-in-the-wool whorehouse, complete with girls and all the trimmings. But lest the story get out of hand I will add that when we went to Dolly's we went as the crew of the *Golden West.* Unless someone sneaked back after our group visitation, I believe none of us ever availed ourselves of the girls' professional services. I could be wrong. We usually trooped in at a fashionable hour, about eight PM, and drank beer with the girls at $1.25 a bottle, which for that time, was a terrible price. Norman Vaara brought his guitar and there was great singing and laughing among the young people there assembled. Perhaps the hallmark of our popularity was the fact that the young ladies always asked us to come back. I recall the girls as being a little on the "hard side," with exotic names like "Tanya," or "Desiree," or "Storm," or some other name that promised night pleasures beyond description. Some of us might have transgressed, but we were all afraid of catching something, and we figured all we could get off a bottle of beer was trench mouth. The girls always sat somewhat sedately and exhibited a lady-like reserve, but for the price of a $1.25 beer one could imagine them pulsating and gyrating in sexual ecstasy. It was a cheaper and safer way to go. I have always felt that a young man who has never been in a whorehouse or a pawn shop isn't worth much; proudly I can say I've been in both.

Our idyllic stay was over in the prescribed time, and we regretfully left the sin and pleasures of Ketchikan to return to the cannery at Waterfall. There followed a satisfying season of hard work and a good salmon pack. We assumed the regular duties of a cannery tender, brailing regularly and doing what else we were told to do. In the course of the season's passing, small things peak in one's mind and enrich the spirit of remembrance. I recall several instances of running in fog that summer. I don't mean haze, I mean dense and pervasive fog which, at times, shrouded the bow of the *Frederick* from view. We were running in constricted spaces; at times a channel's width might be measured in hundreds of yards. In those instances we navigated by "sound-bounce." After practice, a crew member could stand near the bow, forward, and indicate by hand signal to the person at the wheel when he wished the whistle sounded. Following a short blast, the listener/lookout could then rotate his head slightly and, like a bat, pick up the sound after it bounced off the land masses on either side. As the skill developed it was possible to maintain a mid-channel course with a fair degree of accuracy in the most dense of fogs. We all became quite good at it. The use of a lead line to determine depth and the calculations of speed and compass course rounded out our navigational techniques. Both Henry and Norman possessed a tide and current "sense," that made the *Frederick* an outstanding boat upon which to serve.

I would be remiss were I not to mention a singular example of fishing boat handling which occurred toward the end of the 1947 fishing season. A young man of about 30 named Jimmy Young operated the purse seiner, *Rustler,* for Nakat Packing Corporation and was regarded as highly qualified and skilled skipper. We had been brailing traps on the outside in nasty weather when we received an emergency call from the *Rustler* that they were in a "tight situation," and wanted someone to stand by. We were close to their reported position and, of course, responded to their request.

To fully understand the challenges faced by the *Rustler* that day it is necessary to envision the conditions that often existed off the islands lining the west coast of Prince of Wales Island. Dall, Suemez, Baker, and Noyes Islands form a protective bastion running north and south and shelter Prince of Wales Island from the open sea. To the West of these bastion islands there is nothing for thousands of miles save for the rolling gray of the Pacific Ocean which pounds constantly and menacingly against their granite walls. This is where the fish are; therefore, this is a place where fishing boats must go. Fishing in such a spot is a calculated risk that must be constantly evaluated. The skipper, boat, and crew pit their skills against a daily challenge. Usually they emerge successfully and safe, but not always. We rounded a point and were presented with a truly dramatic view.

The day in question was filled with a Southwesterly wind that blasted across the wave tops. The whole world was gray. A heavy rain was wildly slanted by the wind while the waves and tide rips fought each other for domination. Close in to the soaring rock bluffs, the *Rustler* had made several sets filling the boat with a deck load of salmon. Jimmy had made a final set and now was fighting the tides to clear away from the gray walls and the raging ocean that surrounded him. The roar of the sea was constant with the crashing sounds of waves smashing against the island's granite margins, but mostly I remember the gulls. By the hundreds they set to wheeling over the *Rustler,* screaming endlessly in the wind and rain. The laboring engine blasted a smoke plume above the stack which was carried down wind in an instant, while the figures on deck held on to the shrouds or anything else which offered salvation.

On the flying bridge, Jimmy stood with one hand on the wheel and another jamming the throttle lever forward. He was hatless in the driving rain looking forward and aft, but mostly at the granite cliffs a hundred yards to port. Henry held the *Frederick* barely off the scene. It was impossible to get a line to the *Rustler,* she was on her own; at this point we could offer only our closeness, nothing else. The *Rustler,* at last, turned sluggishly away from shore, fighting her way out of captivity by the tide. For a few minutes she hobbyhorsed over the swell, then following our lead, turned north and east toward shelter. In forty minutes we were in quiet water behind the mass of Dall Island. A lot of cussing and laughing was exchanged between the two boats lying close and wallowing together. Henry asked Jimmy Young if he had planned a picnic on the beach or, "had he nothing better to do than tear up a good boat and crew?" Jimmy's boat made a lot of money that day, but everyone knew it had been a close thing. It could well happen again tomorrow or the day after that; such was the nature of the business.

The season ended with a typically high level of activity. Traps were cleared of web and wire then towed to sheltered locations for the winter. Other closing chores were accomplished without incident. We stopped a couple of days in Ketchikan and, in innocence, told the girls at Dolly's Whorehouse good-bye. The *Frederick* made a smooth and gentle journey south with a crew that had worked hard and was now filled with the delicious anticipation of coming home. As soon as the *Frederick* was tied to the dock I called Asa from the littered pay telephone booth outside the Maritime Shipyard office. While I'd been gone, she'd met somebody else. I insisted that we meet for a final talk and we ended up on a wooden bench overlooking the bay somewhere south of Seattle. From where we were, I could look down on the waterway and almost see Fred Foster's houseboat, but my old friend was dead now. There were a lot of things I had to say, but she had made up her mind to say, "Good-bye." I didn't know things that bad ever happened. I can still remember staring at the bench and the initials "C M" in a crude heart carved on its wooden back. I wondered for a moment about who "C" and "M" might be. One thing for sure, at that point in time, the heart was totally inappropriate.

The Season of Forty-Nine

Then, with the passage of a small rocky point, the reality of Rose Inlet sideslipped out of sight. My life in this place was over.

I worked at the shipyard two more weeks and was painting on the *Frederick* one afternoon when the jury-rigged *Hercules*, with her head up high, limped through Salmon Bay on her way to the yard for final repairs. She was rusty and badly beaten up after her encounter with the *Oklahoma*. A boat yard in San Francisco had patched her up a little so she could make it home to Seattle. She chugged right up the channel and guys waved and hollered at her as she went by. There was some message or symbolism about damage control and survival there, but at the time I was in no mood to read it.

There are good years and there are bad years. For me, 1948 was a loser. In retrospect, I think I turned the year up on edge and walked its months like a tightrope, reaching out my arms to seek some kind of balance between what I was, and what I thought I ought to be. There is little point in dwelling on painful times like that; if they help one to grow, so be it. In January of 1949 I knew I wanted to go north again—some kind of homing instinct. Two months later I heard that Norman Vaara was to be the skipper on the *Golden West* that year. I asked him if I could ship on as his deckhand for the 1949 season and he graciously welcomed me back. It was something I really needed. We worked two weeks in the yard shining up the *Golden West* and a couple of other tenders. On an early afternoon in the first part of May, we cleared the Ballard Locks and I was headed back for Waterfall.

I have described the *Golden West* as pretty much a "pedestrian" boat. She was nothing to get excited about, but she had character and some weird idiosyncrasies that, to say the least, were interesting and provocative. She had a one-level deck house and was "UN-fancy," totally lacking the patrician stature of the *Doris E* or the *Frederick C*; she also, quite literally, smelled bad most of the time. We had to get used to that. It really wasn't her fault; it was due to an engine change. I believe the original engine on the *Golden West* had been an old Fairbanks-Morse or small Atlas Imperial. In the late thirties the old engine gave up the ghost and was replaced with a modern six-cylinder Caterpillar diesel. The new engine was a far cry from the behemoths of the old days. It was smaller, easier to operate and maintain, turned at a much greater speed, and lacked the huge flywheel of the marine engines I had known before. To install the new Caterpillar, it had been necessary to remove the engine room's rear bulkhead or wall. This bulkhead separated the engine room from the fish hold in the aft part of the boat. When the bulkhead was reinstalled, that portion conforming to the curvature of the hull was not properly sealed. The result of this ongoing "invitation to odor" became immediately apparent after the first load of fish had filled the hold. The fish gurry ran forward from the fish hold and through the cracks in the ill-fitting bulkhead. From there it sloshed forward under the bilge in the engine room and under the sole or floor of the forecastle where it rested and rotted beneath where we slept.

Although we cleaned the fish hold carefully after each load and poured gallons of chlorine in the bilge to freshen things up, it was to no avail. By mid-season the smell of old fish had permeated our clothes, our bedding and our pores. You could always tell a *Golden West* crew member by the way he smelled. As a consequence we were seldom invited anywhere.

A personnel problem had become apparent before we had even cast off a mooring line. The crew had shared a few beers at the customary farewell party and, by the time wives and friends had gone ashore, the cook was drunk and in his bunk. Fortunately Bob Erling, the cook with whom I had crewed aboard the *Frederick C*, was now my fellow deckhand on the *Golden West*. Although he was reticent to take over, he pitched in with the expectation that the "real cook" would recover in a few hours and assume his responsibilities. We all anticipated the same thing, and since the only liquor aboard was our Aquavit which was locked in the lazarette hatch, the cook's enforced sobriety seemed assured.

NormanVaara was as good a skipper as he had been a mate. There was an air of informality aboard the *Golden West* occasioned by the fact that we were all about the same age, circa 25 to 30, and we had all worked on tenders before. The two-week period of working together ashore had been productive for the boat and the crew. With the exception of the sleeping cook, we left Seattle with the confidence we would have a fine season. Although we carried a hold filled with sundry cannery supplies, the *Golden West* boiled along at a very respectable nine knots. Because of traffic, passage through the Ballard locks had been slow and now, as we headed north through Admiralty Inlet, darkness was gaining the upper hand. Not unexpected, a fog rolled in from the West and slowed us to a crawl. In another hour, we were running blind, at dead slow ahead, in a pervasive blanket of wet blackness. I stood on the foredeck for some time and remember only the cold and an intense concentration as I listened for the sound of the horn on Point Hudson. Norman was at the wheel. Finally there was that faint vibration that was not quite a sound. More listening and head turning, then, after minutes, it grew into the full-fledged voice of a fog horn; Point Hudson lay close off our starboard bow. With a faint glow from the street lights of Port Townsend cutting through the fog, we anchored in quiet water for the night. This was an important time for me. At this writing, after all the years between, I still recall remaining on deck for minutes letting the fog and night wash away the anxiety and uncertainty of the war and the times I'd just been through. Now, I was where I was supposed to be, at the time I was meant to be there. I had only to look forward to another summer doing a job I truly cherished. It was a delightful revelation.

Two days running failed to rouse the cook from a drunken slumber. On a couple of occasions, he had risen to hang on a shroud and pee over the rail, but other than that he remained comatose. We were entranced at his continuing stupor until Norman confronted him and got a good whiff of his breath; the secret was out. Knowing the *Golden West's* smelly reputation, Bob Erling had purchased a season's supply of quart bottles of Mennen's Shaving Lotion. It was a defensive move in the expectation that we just might go back, as

a group, to Dolly's and he didn't want to smell like the boat.

The cook had discovered the stash in the forecastle's medicine chest and was downing Bob's fragrance at the rate of a bottle a day. Needless to say, Erling was furious. While he assumed the cook's duties, the "real cook" was staying drunk on his shaving lotion! Norman concurred with Bob's assessment of the "sonofabitch," and we diverted to Ketchikan where the cook was put ashore still smelling like a barber shop.

We were in a bit of a spot. Bob Erling had signed on as a deckhand, and that's what he wanted to do. In spite of his cooking skills, he said, "To hell with the galley." For a few days, under his direction, I cooked for the crew. With a mutiny about to occur, I was relieved of my duties as chef and replaced by a cook flown out from Ketchikan. In a gastronomic sense, it was a great move. A new tranquillity descended on the vessel as we towed traps and performed the pre-season duties that were assigned. Norman Buschmann was elevated to the position of Skipper of the *Quaker Maid*. We did some hunting and fishing together during "off days" or weekends and remained close friends. The crews on both boats got on well together and we often worked in concert on towing and trap brailing chores.

I have extolled the virtues of the Waterfall Cannery before. It was a great place to work. Personal cleanliness on a boat was always a major concern of mine. Washing facilities aboard consisted of a small sink and usually cold water, but that situation was never a major problem. Though we may have been out for three or four days on various tasks, there were great clean-up facilities at the cannery. The bunkhouse had a number of hot showers and electric clothes washing machines. You hung stuff up in the warehouse to dry. After two or three days of work it was a real treat to go ashore, take a hot shower that scalded the skin and put on a clean set of underwear, jeans and a fresh shirt. The company store at Waterfall had about anything that a crew member really required in the way of personal essentials. In those days everybody smoked, either a pipe or cigarettes, and candy or cold drinks were always available. Games of Pinochle, Gin Rummy, or Cribbage were a constant on the *Golden West* as they were on every other tender afloat. The competition was keen and the quality of the play was very high indeed.

The administration of the cannery was in the hands of experienced and capable men who had spent years in the fishing business. They recognized the needs of cannery crews and were generous and giving in their treatment. On Saturday nights it was easy for a skipper to secure permission to take a cannery tender to Craig for a few hours allowing the crews to taste the fine wine of the "city." Craig was a tiny hamlet, only about two blocks square.

As always, our primary interest was Lib and Jessie's Cocktail Lounge. Our crew always showered and covered ourselves with large doses of shaving lotion to cover the indigenous smell we shared with the *Golden West*. Then, about five or six o'clock on Saturday night, we cranked up the Caterpillar and headed for Craig. On occasions, some of the cannery crew asked permission to accompany us on the journey. Permission was always granted as long as there was space aboard. There was a great deal of merrymaking on these jaunts and the town of Craig was well suited to the task. A couple of restaurants graced the main drag and there was a dance hall with a record machine which intoned over and over, "They all go Native On a Saturday Night." There was a lot of truth in that song. Things could get pretty wild, but if worse came to worse they could shut off the generator and plunge the whole town into instant darkness. It was tough to finish a fist fight with the lights out. There were several liquor stores and an abundance of opportunities for sin. We usually headed back for the cannery about midnight in various stages of inebriation. The world always seemed a little better place because of Craig and Saturday nights.

Cannery tender life presented a very serious "plain and constant danger": that of falling overboard. Such an accident was always a threat on tow boats such as the *Golden West*. Because of the boat's configuration and the necessity to brail fish, it was impossible to construct rails or bulwarks about the entire deck. Around the wheelhouse there was only a slight strake rail perhaps eight to ten inches high, and above that, nothing. On one Craig journey a major problem developed. We departed Waterfall with the crew and a passenger list of ten. After our return to the cannery about midnight, we could confirm only the regular crew and a passenger count of nine. There was no humor in this situation. The missing man was an older cannery worker who had come along for the ride and had not done any heavy drinking. He simply disappeared somewhere on the trip back to Waterfall. The country was rugged, but temperatures were mild and surely not life threatening. If he could reach the beach, he could easily survive. It was useless to attempt anything in the darkness. At first light the *Golden West* began a search which lasted from dawn till dark. We covered the thirteen mile distance several times at slow ahead, blowing the whistle and scanning each side of the channel to no avail. The next day several of us were put ashore by a seine skiff. Though we walked miles of beach on each side of the channel, we found nothing. After a third day of searching the effort was abandoned; the man was never found. It was a tragic and sobering occurrence. Saturday night jaunts were not discontinued as we expected, but a great deal of caution was exercised by the crew, and anyone who drank too much made the return trip in the forecastle or galley.

I have thought many times about a personal "close call" which occurred a month or two following the Craig incident. On the night in question, I was standing a wheel watch and was the only one awake on board the boat. After an hour or so of my watch had

passed, I wanted a cup of coffee. We were far off shore in a slight swell and moving slowly; there was no danger in leaving the wheel for a minute. I went to the port side wheelhouse door with empty coffee cup in hand and, as usual, the damn door was stuck. Rather than put the cup down, maintain my balance, and use both hands, I put my shoulder against the door with some force and it immediately swung open. I lurched out and felt an instant of terror as I nearly went overboard. Had the boat not rolled a little to starboard at that moment, there would have been another drowning. I might have had time for a shout of panic but it is unlikely I would have been heard over the engine sound. It was a terrifying experience which I never repeated and which I've never forgotten.

The season continued in full swing and the run of fish was close to record setting. For a period of two weeks we ran almost constantly, twenty four hours a day, shutting down only to refuel then cranking up to begin emptying traps again. The weather was exceptionally good and the brailing of outside traps progressed without problems. The crew also benefited from a virtual "bonanza" which had fallen in our laps. The Alaskan Fish and Game Department had tagged thousands of pink salmon that year in an attempt to determine migratory patterns. A small, white plastic tag was pinched over the leading edge of the dorsal fin, and any finder who returned the tag was entitled to claim ten cents from the agency. In mid-season, the white tagged salmon began showing up in the traps we were brailing. Soon a virtual flood of tags engulfed us. Being inventive, creative, and greedy, we began harvesting the tags by the hundreds. As the fish were brailed into the boat or scow, a designated "tag man" stood by with a fish pick skewering each tagged fish and removing the plastic tags. All tags were placed in a two pound coffee can under Norman Vaara's bunk, the proceeds to be spent for the "welfare and joy of the crew." When the flow stopped, we redeemed the tags for a commensurate amount of cash and made a weekend trip to Craig. The Great Fish Tag Search of 1949 provided a wild and free weekend of food and drink for the entire crew. In addition, we left Craig carrying many cases of beer which were placed in the lazarette for later consumption. Naturally we were intensely interested in the migratory patterns of *Oncorhynchus gorbuscha,* otherwise known as Pink Salmon. We also felt we had contributed a great deal to the scientific community in its pursuit of the secrets of North American game fish. In the final analysis however, beer, booze, and food had been our motivation and we had been rewarded admirably.

The run of fish seemed unending that year. Though trap fish were the main source of our product, seine and troll fish also contributed to the pack. On several occasions, the *Golden West* towed a barge to a location near the fishing grounds for the purpose of collecting seine fish. Since time was of the essence in seining, many hours were gained when the seiners could deliver to a nearby collection spot. When a barge load of fish was collected, which sometimes occurred in the space of a few hours, the tender would haul that load to the cannery and an additional tender and barge would continue the collection effort.

The procedure was moderately complicated. Seiners were paid on the basis of a fixed amount per fish, but that amount varied depending upon the type of fish caught. At the top of the value chain was the King or Chinook, next, the Silver or Coho, then the Sockeye or Red, followed by the Pink or Humpback and last, came the Chum or Dog Salmon. The individual counting was furnished with a short wooden two-by-four on which were mounted five thumb-operated counters, one for each type of fish. It was his duty to sit by the fish hold on the seine boat and, on the appropriate counters, count the

salmon as they were pitched out of the hold into the collection barge. The counter could "call for fish," that is he could request that "Humpies," or "Reds," be thrown out, but it

The *Copper King*, a cannery tender turned fish buyer, lies hull-down with a deck load of seine fish.

was also essential, that he be able to recognize the type in mid-air, since the seine boat crew would occasionally attempt to substitute a cheaper fish for one of more value. It was a game often played, and a bad "tally-man" could cost the company a lot of money. To further complicate the situation there were usually three or four seine crew members throwing out fish at the same time. If this situation were coupled with the fact that the counting of seine fish went on for extended hours, the difficulty of the task and of being an efficient "tally-man," becomes increasingly clear. The biggest loss occurred when a bright-colored Dog or Chum Salmon was substituted for a Sockeye or Red. If the tally-man caught the scam in mid-air and called out, "Bright Dog!" he was a hero and considered smarter than the fish pitcher who had attempted the larceny. If he missed it, the seine crew suppressed a smile and continued on with the hope of pulling the same scheme again and again. I did pretty well with this, but I'm sure I was tricked occasionally to the delight of the low-level thieves.

...drunks in a seine skiff

The cases of salmon continued to mount in the warehouse and steamers docked almost each week to load the salmon cargo for transit to Seattle. On several occasions, off-duty tender crews were offered the opportunity to "longshore" or load the cargo for a per-hourly wage. It was hard work and the pay from the ship was not great, but it was also a chance to pick up a few dollars for the simple expenditure of muscles and time. On a particular weekend in late August, Norman Buschmann and I, Bob Erling, and two deckhands from the *Quaker Maid* volunteered to help load several thousand cases of salmon on a waiting steamer. We worked hard all afternoon and early evening and, when through, drew our pay. We promptly bought a couple of bottles of whiskey from the ship's Purser at a price which was outrageous. The job of Purser on a steam ship offered many "opportunities;" there were thirsty customers like us everywhere.

We shared our newfound wealth with some others of the crew until, to our dismay, at around ten o'clock that night, we found ourselves out of potables. Craig seemed the only viable option. We knew we could not take a tender so, with bottled reasoning, we commandeered a seine skiff for the thirteen mile trip to the promised land. The seine skiff was a glorified wooden row boat about eighteen feet in length with a small gasping gasoline engine which drove it along at about five knots. It was completely open to the weather and totally inappropriate for the journey. Only an idiot would have conceived of such an undertaking; there were five such individuals immediately available. Amid much bravado and laughter, we started out on our journey in pitch darkness, a lightly falling rain, and rising wind. Miraculously, two and a half hours later we arrived in Craig soaked to the skin. We had rolled and pitched through thirteen miles of bad water on an idiot's expedition and lived. As a justifiable monument to our stupidity, all the liquor stores were closed. For the balance of the night we huddled together, sans alcohol, in the skiff. At dawn we approached the skipper of a native seine boat for a ride back to Waterfall. He agreed to take us home for about what we had intended to spend on booze. The seine skiff was secured astern and, with some weird looks from his crew, we tolerated the trip back to the cannery with empty pockets, empty dreams, empty heads and hangovers. Thankfully the Superintendent was unaware of our adventure.

The *Yes Bay*

An old boat with the heart of a lion.

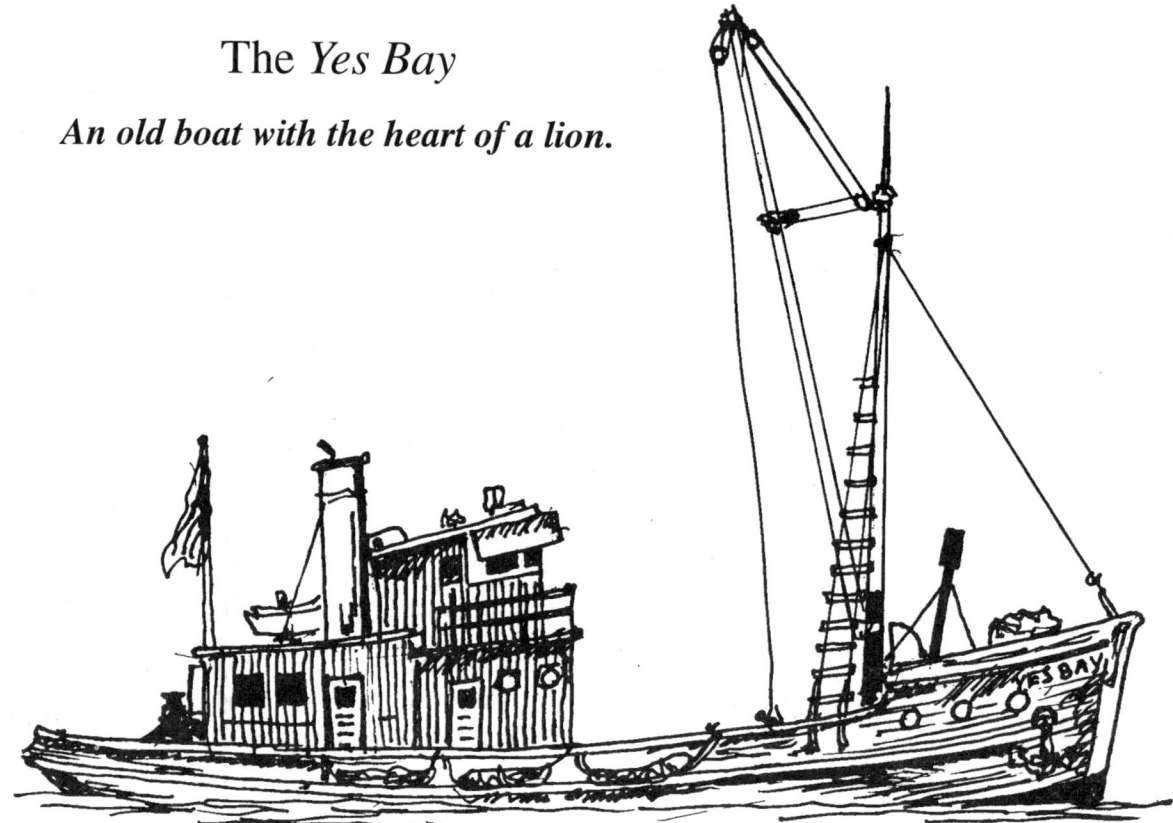

The season was nearly over but a major drama was still waiting in the wings to be played out. Waterfall Cannery had lent the ancient cannery tender *Yes Bay* to a company which was experiencing a huge glut of troll fish at a fish buying station near Waterfall. These troll-caught fish were beautiful large King Salmon which were iced down and packed in large wooden boxes for transportation to Prince Rupert, British Columbia, a run of some 150 miles to the South. They were prime fish and constituted a cargo of very high value.

To those of us in the tender fleet, the *Yes Bay* was a source of derision. She had been built in 1912, and the *Ship Register* at that time, listed her as the "gas screw Lummi." She was originally equipped with a gasoline engine, but later fitted out with a Metz and Weiss diesel engine of early German design. Some claimed that this engine had been removed from a World War I German submarine but, through research, this has been pretty well ruled out. Had this been true, it would have formed a rational argument for the fact that the Kaiser lost the war. Before being acquired by Nakat Packing Corporation, the *Yes Bay* had huffed and puffed her way around Alaska for nearly four decades. My dad had suffered early career experiences with the boat and its engine which he referred to as that "Goddam rats and mice engine." He felt pretty much the same about the Metz and Weiss as he did about the direct reversible diesels that had, at times, plagued his career. The *Yes Bay's* engine was primitive and given to blasting out large pieces of soot and carbon when started; a broom was a constant requirement when she was underway. The vessel and its power were food for jokes and laughter. That would soon change.

I believe it was on a weekend that we found ourselves in a small protected inlet just north of Cape Chacon and my old nemesis, Dixon Entrance. Norman Vaara had noticed a falling glass indicating the possible approach of bad weather and we had chosen the "better part of valor." Find some place to hide until it's over! At the same time, seventy five miles north at Noyes Island the *Yes Bay* was being loaded with wooden boxes of iced King Salmon destined for Prince Rupert B.C. Jay Ellis, then Skipper of the *Satrania*, another fish packer, assisted in the loading at the time and stated in a recent telephone call: "The *Yes Bay*, on her last trip, was loaded with something close to 28,000 pounds below and close to 12,000 pounds of boxed fish on deck, most of this forward of the house to adjust her trim." In a word, the old lady was loaded to the hilt. In addition, she carried some steel drums aft filled with lubricating oil for which she had an insatiable appetite.

The weather had grown into full fledged ugliness when we heard the first radio message asking for help. She had passed our place of refuge a couple of hours before and had stumbled into the churning wickedness which Dixon Entrance and the Cape had become. Dan Starkweather, the skipper of the *Yes Bay*, reported the lashings had broken and the deck load had shifted to starboard creating a severe list which was threatening to sink her. The heavy boxes had become "loose cannons," smashing into her gunwales, then splintering into pieces. He also advised that an aging deck hand had passed out and was comatose on the wheelhouse deck, barely breathing from a suspected heart attack. Before the message was finished, our engine was started and Norman Vaara ordered us forward to raise the anchor. In ten minutes, with the throttle lever to the stops, we were making for Cape Chacon.

Through the spray and rain we saw the *Yes Bay* first from about a half mile away, just south of the Cape. The weather was as vicious as I had seen. Wind tore off the wave-tops, hurling them against the wheelhouse, threatening to smash in the windows. Visibility was

so bad the windows had to be lowered part way. In seconds we were soaked and sea water was sloshing back and forth across the wheelhouse sole. We had taken heavy water from the beam seas and the galley, aft of the wheelhouse, was awash. The weather could best be summed up by Norman's comment, "Ain't this a son-of-a-bitch!"

When we closed to within about two-hundred yards to lee of the *Yes Bay,* it was plain to see that her situation was desperate. My vision of her is as clear today as it was then. She was wallowing in a maelstrom sea. Her deck load had shifted forcing her to list severely to starboard. The water around her was littered with hundreds of the heavy wooden salmon boxes, some intact, and some broken into splinters with the large iced Chinooks floating around them. Many of the cases had lodged crazily against the *Yes Bay's* starboard railings, a log-jam of weight that was beginning to turn her over. Seas were breaking over her stern, and two large steel drums aft of her cabin had broken loose and were rolling side to side threatening to crush anything in their way.

It was obvious she had to execute a 180 degree turn and head back the way she had come. The timing for the turn would be absolutely critical. To save the boat, she had to be brought about between swells. Vaara and Starkweather confirmed the plan by radio and we pulled up about two hundred yards to windward to stand by and offer whatever small shelter we could.

The engineer was standing by in our engine room while our cook, was in the galley attempting to salvage some order from the welter of pots and pans and crockery that now littered the galley floor. Norman was at the wheel and Bob and I were glued to the half open windows of the wheelhouse, drenched with sea water and immersed in a drama we could scarcely believe. We waited for one minute, then two, then perhaps three or four, watching the mountainous sea for any semblance of a momentary calm. Then it seemed that there was a slight flattening and the *Yes Bay* began her struggle to turn and survive.

The skipper put her helm far over to lessen the turning time and she began to swing fairly quickly, her rails under water from the weight of the cases jammed against her starboard gunwale. She had turned 90 degrees when a huge crest rolled under the *Golden West* and rushed ahead to hit the *Yes Bay* full abeam. It seemed a body-blow she couldn't withstand. The full force of the breaking wave rolled the stricken tender full over on her starboard side. The remaining heavy salmon cases cascaded across her near-vertical deck into a welter of foam and debris, while the filled oil drums astern smashed into her starboard gunwales and bounced overboard.

The sight would be carved forever in the minds of the three of us who watched.

There were no words as the bow of the *Yes Bay* rolled under and raised her stern clear of the water. For a seemingly endless time she poised there with the huge green-yellow propeller slowly churning the air, while her mast and boom, mounted forward, laid on the passing swell like a head on a pillow. I saw the encrusted bottom of her rudder and skeg and knew she was going down.

For perhaps thirty seconds she lay on the surface like a dead bird rolling in the debris of her own making: gutted salmon, smashed boxes floating bits of line, and rusted tin cans. I still see the floating oak bucket which had held her heaving line. In the midst of the violence of this place, these moments seemed a noiseless, breath-holding time; something like a death watch.

Then there was the miracle. Her stern lowered slowly into the water where it belonged and the huge propeller once more began turning the water into a green-whiteness. She shook and rose very slowly like the bag-woman she was, then she wallowed about finishing the turn, and headed slowly back towards us and towards safety. Her decks were swept clean, shedding cascades of white water beam to beam, while the black smoke and cinders trailed from her stack and vanished in the wind. In two hours, we had crawled together back to the safety of the bay. In the plan of things, it was hard to define who was the saved, and who was the savior!

Everything else was anti-climactic. The engine room on the *Yes Bay* had shipped two feet of water, but the old "Rats and Mice" diesel had a compression base and the engine would probably have continued to bang away totally submerged and upside down! The galley was a shambles, but was set right again after some hours of brooms and mops had filled a GI can with broken crockery and wet playing cards. Two port side 4x4 oak strakes had been snapped off when the oil drums went over the side, but other than drying out, the *Yes Bay* was little the worse for wear.

The ailing deck hand had indeed been unconscious, but only from the effects of severe sea-sickness; he recovered after a day's rest in the quiet backwater of the small bay. If memory serves me right, both the *Golden West* and the *Yes Bay* were back in harness by Monday, but that afternoon would be the most memorable of all. I never laughed at the *Yes Bay* after that. Before our eyes she had risen from the sea like a Phoenix to the disbelief of all of us who had been there to witness her triumph. Her bones are now bleaching on the shore of Gastineau Channel outside Juneau. Before she died, someone had changed her name to the *Tongass Queen*... I think it's bad Karma to change the name of a vessel. A small landslide has covered part of her but a boat like that has a soul that goes on forever.

The year of 1949 will be forever marred by a dreadful sadness which took place close to the end of the fishing season. Kathy Brazeau, the lovely young girl whom I met while a teenager at Lakeside School had married the son of Mr. Haakon Friele, Chief Executive Officer of Nakat Packing Corporation. Departing, after visiting a company cannery, a tragic take-off accident occurred. Kathy, Mrs. Haakon Friele, two passengers, and both pilots of the company plane were killed. The accident cast a pall over the entire Nakat organization and indeed over the whole of Alaska.

About a week later the *Golden West* was assigned a final task for the year. We were to go to an abandoned cannery site at Rose Inlet and empty a storage building of some aged machinery. We were told to take our time, and were assured that there was no rush about the job. When it was finished, we were to return to Waterfall, pick up some provisions for the trip home, and return to Seattle. Rose Inlet was only twenty-five miles south of the cannery, but we had never stopped there. The nautical chart displayed the inlet as deeply indenting the East side of Dall Island in Tlevak Strait; that was a masterful piece of understatement. We left the cannery early, just shortly after dawn and, running slowly, reached the Inlet about mid-day. For September the weather was phenomenal. Since dawn, there had been a cloudless sky and warm, bright sunshine. Not being completely confident with the charted soundings, we transited the narrow entrance channel slowly until it widened into a small bay of incomparable beauty and tranquillity. The deserted cannery lay on the North side of the bay and its buildings, rusting and dilapidated, had begun to return to the primal state of their birth. It was a sedentary and defenseless collection of rusted roofing and weathered timber which, in its way, seemed to belong there. More a memory than a structure, it could never detract from the exquisite scene that surrounded us.

The margins of the quiet bay were lined with virginal, small-stone beaches, that stretched back to a thick growth of mixed timber and dried underbrush. Several small streams emptied quietly onto the shores defining their pathways with trout-laden waters which sparkled with an amber clarity. Covered with an essence of spruce and fir, the hills rose at an alarming angle, stretching the neck back, until they topped themselves with granite reaches which appeared "hard lined" against the blue of the afternoon sky. Gulls slowly circled the green and shadow-silvered water, unobtrusive and uttering few cries. Rose Inlet seemed to dwell in a state of infinite peace. That was its crowning grace. In spite of the intrusion of the old cannery, there was a blissful feeling of aloneness there.

We anchored quietly not too far from shore and spent the late afternoon inspecting the cannery buildings and assessing the job before us. A considerable collection of old rusting machinery was to be dragged to a large hole in the floor of the cannery building and thence dropped to the graveled tide flats below where it would be degraded by the tide. Since there was no hurry, we hiked about the bay that afternoon inspecting the beaches which were rich with the vestiges of deer and black bear prints. We took the skiff back to the boat, drank a couple of "fish tag beers," and watched evening descend in an unbroken silence. There were some rustling sounds from a near beach after dark, and just before I fell asleep I heard the softness of an owl's cry. Beside those sounds, the world here was filled with only the stillness of the stars.

Morning came with a surprising warmth, promising a repeat of the magnificent weather of the day before. The smell of the morning forest permeated the air, sweetening the scent of early coffee. Drinking from a hot navy mug on the stern, I could see several deer grazing in a field of saw-grass a quarter of a mile away. After breakfast we rowed ashore and began the task of clearing the building of its rusted contents. Most of it was ancient canning machinery hearkening back to the early days when salmon cans were formed by hand, one at a time. The old artifacts merely confirmed the isolation and solitude that resided here. We worked steadily most of the day and steeled ourselves for a swim in the late afternoon. The water was chilling cold with a diamond clearness which magnified the texture of colored stones on the bottom, fifteen feet below. Then, once again, the peace of evening blanketed the world around us.

We worked slowly and steadily for four days in Indian summer weather which transfigured the land and sea. On the last afternoon, in a dust-filled finale, I pushed a large broom across the broad expanse of ancient flooring. Everything had been thrown down the hole and lay in a rust-red conical pile which would be slowly eaten in the years of coming tides. During these days I sensed an approaching end to the wonder years I'd known on these boats and in Alaska.

I don't remember any overwhelming sorrow in that. I recall only an acceptance of the probability that I would not return here coupled with a wondering about what lay ahead. The sea, the land and some wooden hulls had granted me the gift of a new beginning, a new confidence, and a new strength to do different things in a new and different place. I had found a catalyst which dispelled the anxiety and uncertainty that had held me for awhile. The remedy was a simple mixture of wooden boats, good friends and the adventure of a shining sea. That night we shared the last of the fish tag beer. I slept very well.

Dawn broke clear and windless but with high, "mare's tail" clouds hinting of weather to come. The dew of morning covered everything with a coating of lustrous beads, while a rose-colored mist screened off the entrance channel. It would burn off in an hour. In this silent place, the clink of plates and white cups cracked against the morning quiet. Too soon the engine's rumble began and Bob and I went forward to raise the anchor. The chain rattled slowly through the hawse pipe, then the hook broke through the surface, shattering the iridescent sea like a piece of colored glass. We were a group of caustic, profane kids, not given to the romantic; but I sensed a universal reticence to leave the peace of that enchanted place.

The *Golden West* turned slowly toward the entrance. In a dead-slow exit filled with dignity, we scarcely rippled the surface with our parting. The entrance mist was rising in the morning sun. With a cup of hot coffee I stood on the back deck committing the inlet's loveliness to memory. Then, with the passage of a small rocky point, the reality of Rose Inlet sideslipped out of sight. My life in this place was over.

We left behind only a thinning mantle of early morning diesel smoke which slowly rose then vanished before my cup was empty.